TEACHING GOLF
TO SPECIAL
POPULATIONS

A publication of
Leisure Press.

P.O. Box 3, West Point, NY 10996

Copyright © 1984 Leisure Press
All rights reserved. Printed in the U.S.A.

Library of Congress Cataloging in Publication Data
Main entry under title:

Teaching golf to special populations.

Written by DeDe Owens and others.
Bibliography: p.
1. Golf—Study and teaching—Addresses, essays,
lectures. 2. Sports for the handicapped—Study and
teaching—Addresses, essays, lectures. I. Owens, DeDe.
GV965.T3 1984 796.352'02408 84-5772
ISBN 0-88011-036-8

TEACHING GOLF TO SPECIAL POPULATIONS

DeDe Owens, Ed.D.

LEISURE PRESS
NEW YORK

Acknowledgments

The authors wish to acknowledge the following people for their help throughout the preparation of this manuscript: Susie Knott and Nina Seaman for their secretarial assistance; Carol Davis and Barbee Bancroft for their illustrations; Mike Orlansky for his help on the visually impaired; and Linda Bunker for her guidance, patience and editorial assistance.

    This book is the work of six individuals who have shared their knowledge of the game of golf and the pleasures of working with special people. But it really represents the collective influence of many great teachers and golfers. We wish to extend our most sincere appreciation to our friends and teachers from the NGF, LPGA and PGA.

The Authors

It's not always easy to
figure out who we are
or where we're going . . .

E. Sequil

To those who have
been there — especially "Casper"

Thank you

Contents

Foreword

This book will leave a lasting impression on each individual who reads it. The analysis of the golf swing and practice ideas will help golf teachers as well as 20-handicappers. But most importantly, the messages in this book are many—about golf, about people, and about sharing.

The golf information in *Teaching Golf to Special Populations* provides a synthesis of the most current techniques of golf instruction. The laws, principles and preferences (modified from Wiren) and the short game approach of Johnson and Johnstone provide a simple method for understanding the mechanics of the swing itself. The historical analysis of the swing is an intriguing and insightful chapter on the adaptations which the environment and club design caused on the nature of the swing and sets the scene for the modifications which may be needed for individuals with handicapping conditions.

In addition to the excellent information on the golf swing itself, the teaching strategies and communication aids will be helpful to all teachers. The ideas presented in these chapters focus on the importance of analyzing the special needs of each student. The goal setting techniques and motivational ideas will be useful in many situations.

This book may have its greatest impact on how each of us feels about the game of golf itself and about ourselves. Golf has the potential to make a major contribution to the quality of lives for individuals with handicapping conditions. This book will help you become more comfortable and qualified to help each person. The authors possess tremendous expertise both as golfers and as teachers. Through their guidance and insights the true challenges and pleasures of golf can be available for everyone.

Linda K. Bunker, Ph.D.
Chairperson
Department of Health and
Physical Education
University of Virginia

Preface

Efforts have been made in the past decade to foster increased national awareness of the need and importance of sport and recreation for individuals with handicapping conditions. Along with the recognition of importance is the belief that each individual, handicapped or non-handicapped, should be able to pursue recreational activities of his choice.

As golf instructors, we must support the belief in the importance of golf for all individuals by increasing the opportunity for the handicapped to play golf. Increased opportunity can be gained in several ways. We must raise the public's awareness of the potential for participation in golf by a wide variety of individuals with handicapping conditions. Golf courses and practice ranges must be physically and psychologically accessible to individuals with handicaps. Quality instruction geared to the needs of the particular handicap must be provided.

To work effectively with a handicapped individual requires that the teacher have an understanding of the disability in general and of special teaching needs in particular. The initial reaction of most teachers faced with the task of teaching these individuals without such understanding is one of fear, dismay, threat and anxiety. These feelings create a barrier between the teacher and the student, blocking communication and therefore a level of awareness and understanding necessary for an effective teacher-learner interaction.

The intent of this manual is to present the experienced and inexperienced golf instructor with a practical guide for teaching special populations. Included are the physically impaired, mentally retarded, visually impaired, and hearing impaired. It is hoped this manual will enable the teacher to create a bridge rather than a barrier between themselves and any handicapped individual seeking instruction. The bridge will provide the basis for effective communication and therefore, a productive teacher-learner relationship. Working with individuals who have handicapping conditions can be viewed as an exciting challenge to your creativity and imagination as teachers anxious to share the joys of golf.

Individual golfers are the focus of all golf instruction. A person with a limiting condition is not a "handicapped person"—he is a golfer who has a handicapping condition which may or may not affect his ability to develop a fine golf game. It would therefore be preferable never to refer to "the handicapped" or a "handicapped individual." However, common language usage and simplicity may allow this. The important factor is to always remember that you work with a valuable, unique individual each time you teach.

DeDe Owens

PART 1

Introduction

CHAPTER 1

What Golf Did For Me

by Corbin Cherry

Anyone reading a title like the one above would think the author had a special relationship with golf. This is no doubt true, but in my case the story rests not in the performance and certain levels and achievements of excellence in the sport, but rather in the mere act of playing the game at any performance level. This is the relationship I will address in the following pages.

In 1969 I became a professional dreamer while I was lying on the floor of the jungle somewhere in a remote area of South Viet-Nam. I was the victim of a land mind explosion that left me without the lower part of my left leg. I say that I was a professional dreamer because all that I could think about, lying there, was the possibility that I might not be able to play golf again with my leg gone. I did not think about working, I did not think about running and walking again; all that flooded my mind was that I might have to give up golf.

My basic thoughts were that I just wanted to be able to play golf again. At first I was not concerned with how well I would play, but just that I would be able to play. Yet somewhere in the deep recesses of my mind I knew there would come a day when I would not settle for "just playing golf." I would want to play better and better. I believe this was the beginning of the healing process for me.

As I lay there in the hospital thinking about how much I had enjoyed the sport, I began to devise methods of how I could compensate for what had happened to me. I remembered again the day I was wounded and how I thought I would never play golf again. I remembered the medic who was tending my wounds while crying profusely. "Can you believe this?" I said to him. "How am I going to play golf on one leg?"

He turned from his work on my leg, wiped the tears away and started to smile. "Chaplain, if there is a way, you will find it." He was right. Those hours and that day are long past and those feelings have given way to the realization that most things are possible to most people if they really want to accomplish them.

It is true that the accomplishment of excellence in the game was and is a real "turn on" to me, but the *real* significance lies in the fact that I can play golf again. This kind of feeling not only occurs with golf but with any activity that is above the natural flow of life. For instance, to a person who has been unable to walk for an extended period of time, just walking is not only a miracle but is far more than "just" walking. It is a dream come true. There have been only a few times when I have played golf that I did not remember the feelings that I had lying there in the jungle, wondering about the possibilities of playing golf ever again. After my injury, I needed to have dreams and fantasies about what I could do and where I could go. Golf allowed some of those dreams and fantasies to come true.

Still I feel that the greatest part golf played in my life (or maybe in readjusting my life) was the increased level of self confidence; the knowledge that I could accomplish a definite task. Again, to me, perfecting the level of competence is and will always be an ongoing goal, but the sheer development of physical capabilities to play the game gave me what I needed, a goal and a success rate. True the goals and success rates changed as I began to better myself, but the victory is no sweeter today, when I have a par round, than it was when I stood there in my old high school football stadium and hit those first golf shots after the loss of my leg. When I first swung that nine iron and hit that little white ball, I was ready for a thrill and it was there—boy, was it there.

Golf has allowed me to enjoy myself physically, as has snow skiing. Before my amputation I was a jogger, and was running about ten miles a day. It was obvious to me as I was recuperating that I would not be running that far and that long again. So I tried to channel the energies I had used in running into a different area of my life; golf and skiing were to become the recipients of those energies. I can walk around a golf course today and remember when I used to run around the golf course, but I also realize that as much as I enjoyed the jogging, I enjoy seeing the flight of the little white ball after I hit a golf shot, (as long as the shot is accurate) even more.

Golf has allowed me to enjoy myself physically, mentally and emotionally. It has given me emotional highs with the achievement of definite confidence levels. It has allowed me the joy of meeting new people and the sheer joy and nearly indescribable pleasure of being able to witness to the fact that it is the spirit in the human mind and body that determine its limits. I have seen men with no hands hold a golf club in the bend of their arms and with great effort not only swing at, but hit the ball. The results of the swing may not have been great by some standards, but judged by the internal values and hopes of the person hitting the shots, they were as good as the best. I have watched the smiles that followed those shots and they can only be characterized as "highs." The incredible part of all of this is that for most of them, sports (in this case golf) is one of only a few things that cause a smile inside and out—pleasure for sure.

Golf has allowed me the chance to share with others the joy and frustration of the sport. It has given all of these elements to me from just watching others participating in the game.

In athletics we talk about the thrill of victory and the agony of defeat. Those moments are as real as is this day in which we live. But I believe they are intensified in the life of a disabled person. The defeats come to us all if we hang around long enough. For the disabled, the depth of defeat is overshadowed by the joy of what would be viewed by some as a very small victory, but to them is a "mountain top experience." Victory for many may just be participating in the sport. How well I remember those feelings of victory.

It has always been obvious to me that the old adage of "no one will remember the person who finishes second" is not always true; for time and time again there have been people, myself included, who did not win the match but won the game simply because they played. This alone can produce a winner's attitude in those of us who play the game. Another gift of learning from golf.

It has been for me, as a handicapped person, a real joy to be as involved with sports after my amputation as I was before. Being able to participate, understand the thrill of victory and become more aware are some of the resources that golf has granted me.

Golf for most people who are "normal" has its ups and downs, but I believe it means more to someone who has overcome a disability than it does for the "normal" person. You are expected to accomplish certain levels when you are "normal" and others when you are disabled. It seemed to me I tried a bit harder after I lost my leg than I did before to perfect my game. It's as if I had to prove a point to "normal" people and to other people who had lost some part of their body. So in fighting the odds and winning the battle, the thrills are there and so are the directions that are so important in this life.

Golf as I have said, has allowed me many areas in which to feel good, but it is so nice to be able to go to the golf course after a mentally tiring day and find relief. I can take it there and leave it there. I spell relief, G-O-L-F.

I once watched a group of handicapped people trying to hit some golf shots. I tried to relate to their physical problems, but except for a very few I could not know how they felt. Still, they were normal in the reaction to the game. They had frustration and they had joy, and the joy was the ultimate experience for them. The frustration would pass, but the joy would be remembered. Golf again had allowed me some great feelings from just watching other people attaining a mountain-top experience. I sat there and I penned the following words.

There are times when we are gifted by life; this day is a case in point. To not know but a fraction of the life that we lead and to never be able to accomplish the insurmountable task of being anything but a small part in the very complex world in which we live, we are thrown bits and pieces of life itself; and then we realize that the prize goes not to catcher but rather to the source from whence the prize emanates. As the catcher slowly begins to grow and life becomes of more and more value, to him or to her, they realize that time has allowed the greatest of gifts to occur. That gift is that the receiver may one day ascend to the top of the marble cliff and will in that day throw bits and pieces of knowledge, hope and above all love to still another catcher waiting his turn to climb the mountain. The gift of life is that we get a chance to climb that mountain.

Golf has allowed me the greatest of gifts: freedom of body, mind, and above all, spirit. I could ask for no more.

PART 2

Instructional Techniques For Golf

CHAPTER 2

Model For Golf Instruction

by DeDe Owens and Carol Johnson

Golf is a sport activity which lends itself to participation by all segments of the population. Because of the inherent nature of the game, it may be played both socially, where the emphasis is on friendly recreation and not necessarily on shooting a super score, and competitively, in which there may be intrinsic or extrinsic motivation to shoot the best score. The game may be played by individuals or a group. Within a group, individuals may be participating for a variety of personal reasons while still participating together.

For individuals with handicapping conditions, golf provides an exceptional activity for participation within their own capabilities and limitations. The progressive skill opportunities which can be established, based on the individual needs, fosters success and challenges with minimal frustration and can aid in the personal progress of each handicapped individual. These individuals want to challenge themselves and to be challenged by others. In addition, the golf (USGA) handicapping system permits all individuals to compete together regardless of skill levels. The nature of the game allows modification to meet individual needs through adaptation of techniques and equipment.

Once the individual has expressed an interest and desire to learn golf, it is up to you, the instructor, to find and establish a means of communicating the complexities of the game in their simplest terms. Each instructor must assess each student's movement patterns and adapt the swing mechanics to meet the individual's needs. In order to do this, and to maximize an individual's potential, it is necessary for the instructor to

• have an understanding of mechanical principles
• be a skilled observer
• be able to interpret the observed swing style
• prescribe and communicate the pattern of movement that will foster individual skill development.

In working with the handicapped, the movement patterns may or may not deviate from those generally observed. However, the instructor must have an understanding of the swing principles to make any adaptation which may be necessary.

A skilled instructor must understand the golf swing. This requires that some frame of reference be established for assessing the swing. Unfortunately, the instructional phase of golf is not a "canned package," but is in a perpetually changing state. The swing is constantly being analyzed by teachers, players and sports analysts. As a result, there are almost as many approaches and theories as there are golf teachers. Accordingly, there is great confusion among teachers and players regarding appropriate motor patterns for swinging a golf club.

The confusions and controversies over the golf swing are due not so much to the mechanics of golf, the theories or methods of presentation, as to the fragmented interpretations and comparisons by the golfer. Often the confusion arises from isolating various mechanical aspects without viewing their interaction within the total swing motion.

During the past decade three major organizations—the Professional Golfers of America (PGA), the Ladies Professional Golf Association (LPGA), and the National Golf Foundation (NGF)—have undertaken a unified effort to promote and upgrade the instruction of golf throughout the country. From their efforts and the work of Gary Wiren, former director of the PGA Educational Servies and current PGA director of club and professional relations, a model for golf instruction has been introduced. This model has become known as "Laws, Principles and Preferences."[1]

Wiren's model was formulated from the basic laws of physics which affect the flight of a golf ball when it is struck *(results)* and the application of the mechanical principles used in swinging a golf club *(causes)*. The model incorporates cause and effect relationships in understanding and communicating the mechanics of the golf swing. This model provides a rational and logical approach to the golf swing through the application of mechanical principles which may be modified in a variety of ways. The model does not dictate the manner in which the principles must be applied, thereby allowing for individualized instructional approaches. With this strength, Wiren's model is most appropriate for consideration in working with the handicapped. The following section presents the framework of Wiren's model.

---

1.   Wiren, Gary. *"The Search for the Perfect Teaching Method."* NGF, ES-7, 1976.

Laws, Principles and Preferences

Wiren's definitions of the ball flight Laws, Principles and Preferences are as follows:

- Laws are dynamic in that there is a range within them which produces cause and effect and therefore must be dealt with in each individual stroke.
- Principles are the first cause or force with direct relationship and influence on the laws.
- Preferences are the act of choosing. . .that must relate to the principles.

When we consider the Laws, Principles and Preferences, simply stated, they will become the model for our comparisons of the various parts of the full swing, short shot and putting.

Laws are those things that happen to a ball in flight whether you are Jack Nicklaus, Nancy Lopez-Melton, Tommy Watson or Patty Berg. They occur whether you are young or old, short or tall, blessed with special talent or just an average athlete. The ball doesn't know who is applying force to it, or at what angle or direction, or where it is being struck. It simply follows the laws of ball flight without regard to its striker. The following are the five ball flight laws:

- Speed—the velocity with which the clubhead is traveling—influences the distance the ball will be propelled (slower speed = shorter distance; faster speed = longer distance).
- Path—the direction in which the clubhead is moving—will largely determine the direction in which the ball will start out (for a right handed golfer, path straight to the right of target line = push; and path straight to the left of target line = pull).
- Face—the degree at which the surface of the club-face running on a vertical axis is at right angles to the intended line—will influence the accuracy of the ball's flight along the line (for a right handed golfer an open or closed club-face at impact puts spin on the ball: open face = slice; and closed face = hook).
- Angle of Approach—the angle formed by the descending line of the clubhead on the downswing—influences the trajectory and affects the distance the ball will travel. Angle of approach also includes the point of contact on the ball by the club—above, below or in the center of the ball (hits above center = a very low ball; hits below center = high hit).
- Position on the club face influences additional spins. They are put on the ball when it is contacted by the face of the club and vary with the position toward the toe or heel—top or bottom of the face. This is the *ONE* law that is very unlikely to be controlled by the player.

Principles are those parts of a golf swing that must be present. Let us take a few of the twelve principles listed in the model as an example: the grip, the timing and the plane. Every swing must have a grip. A grip may be with one hand, two hands, ten fingers or less, or a prosthetic device (an artificial arm). But it is still a grip. Timing involves the sequence of the swing beginning with the hand, arms, shoulders, and lower body on the back swing and reversing the order on the swing on the forward sequence. Every swing has a plane. A tall, lean person is usually going to have a much more upright plane than a short-statured person. Inflexibility and bulges in the stomach are a few of the influences that can cause a swing plane to flatten or resemble a merry-go-round.

Throughout the history of golf there has been a constant search for the perfect combination of preferences within the principles, that will produce the "perfect swing." The search will go on, for just as there is no "one body build, set of talents or mind" for all men or women, there is no one swing that will be perfect for everyone. Each individual will have to combine the principles with his own personal preference combinations to produce the most effective and efficient swing for himself.

The principles and potential preferences of the golf swing that will be emphasized in this book can be developed into pre-swing (prior to beginning swing motion) and in-swing (during swing motion). The principles are presented below with diagrams of the preferences.

Pre-Swing:
- Grip—Holding the club.

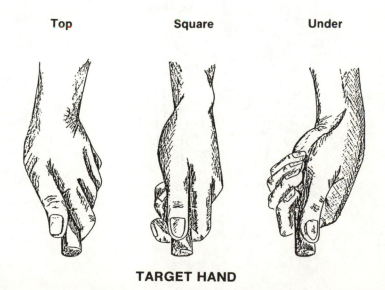

Top   Square   Under

TARGET HAND

Figure 2.1 Grip Preferences

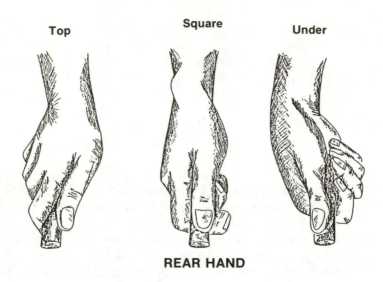

REAR HAND

Figure 2.2 Grip Preferences (Continued)

- Aim—Placing the club behind the ball and aligning the stance and body to the target line.

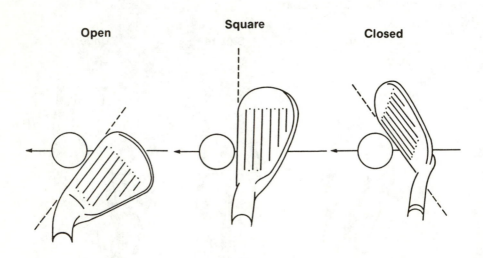

Figure 2.3 Blade Alignment Preferences

Shoulder Alignment

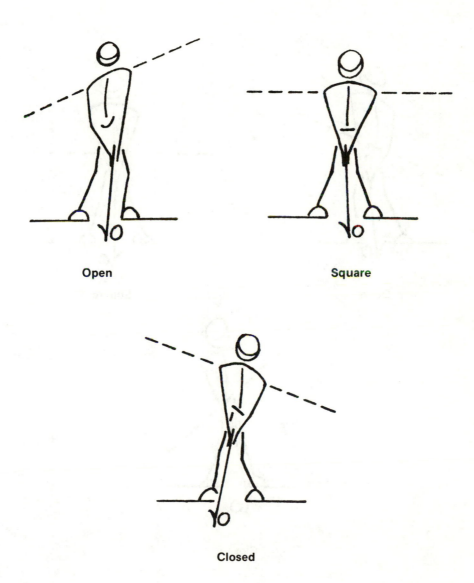

Open   Square

Closed

Figure 2.4 Alignment Preferences (Continued)

Hip Alignment

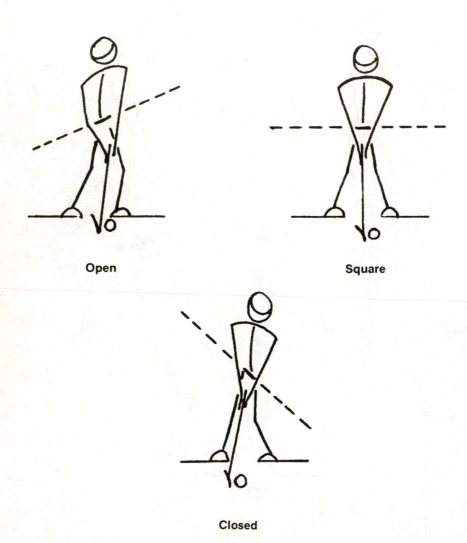

Open

Square

Closed

Figure 2.5 Alignment Preferences (Continued)

Feet Alignment

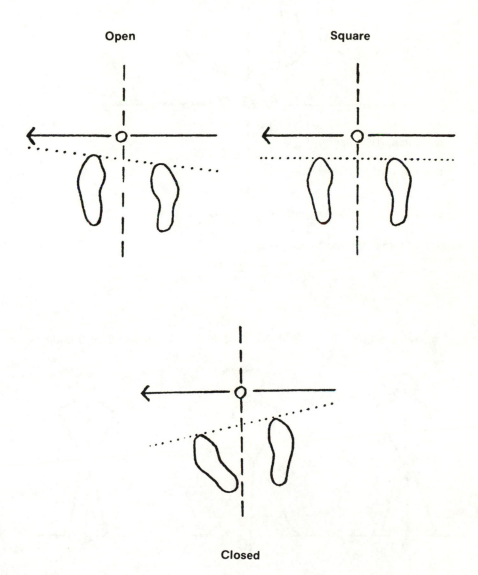

Figure 2.6 Alignment Preferences (Continued)

- Set-up—Choosing the placement of the ball, width of the stance, body posture, weight distribution, and balance of the body.

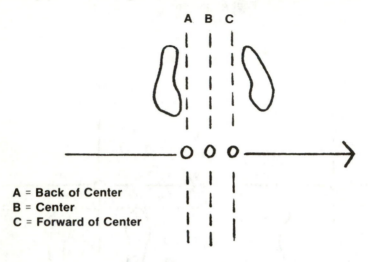

A = Back of Center
B = Center
C = Forward of Center

Figure 2.7 Ball Position Preferences

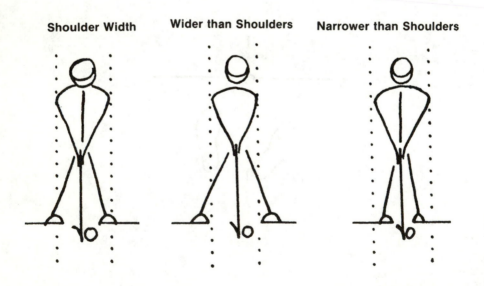

Figure 2.8 Stance Preferences

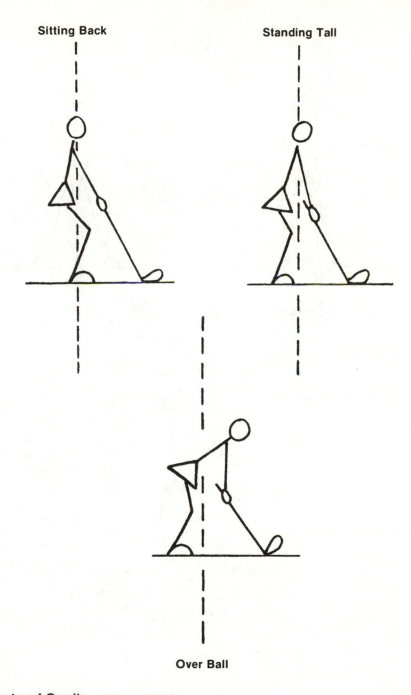

Figure 2.9 Upper Body Posture Preferences

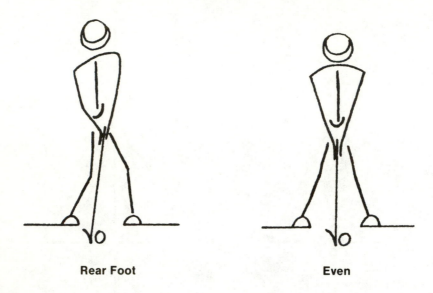

Rear Foot   **Even**

Target Foot

Figure 2.10 Target-Rear Foot Weight Distribution Preferences

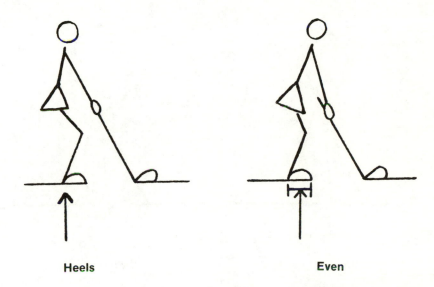

Heels　　　　　　　　　　　　**Even**

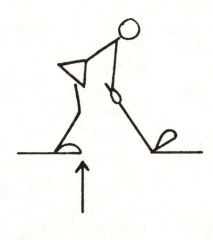

Toes

Figure 2.11 Heel-Toe Weight Distribution Preferences

In-Swing:
- Arc Width—The radius of the swing equals the arm length plus the club length.

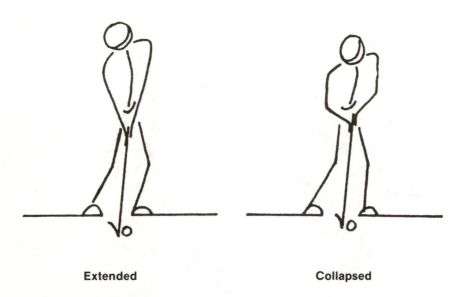

Extended   **Collapsed**

Figure 2.12 Width of Arc Preferences

- Position of the Hands at the Top—The position of the club relating to face making it open, closed or square to the target line.

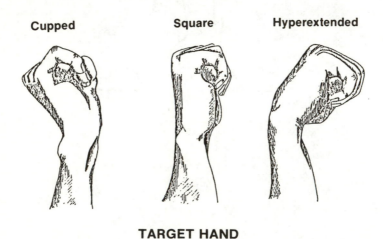

Cupped   **Square**   **Hyperextended**

TARGET HAND

Figure 2.13 Position at the Top Preferences

Hyperextended   **Square**   **Cupped**

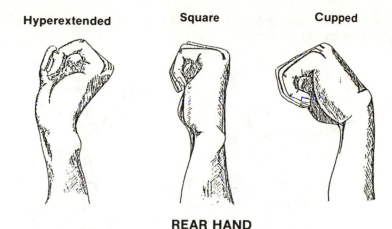

REAR HAND

Figure 2.14 (Continued) Position at the Top Preferences

- Length of the Arc—The circumstance of the swing, how far back and forward it travels.

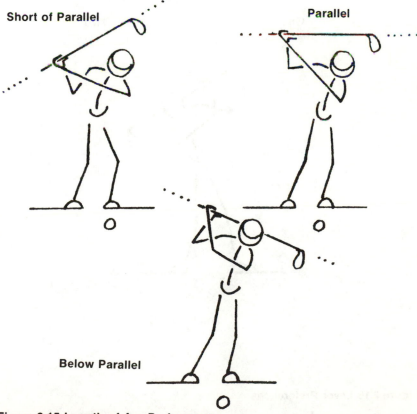

Figure 2.15 Length of Arc Preferences

- Lever—The cocking of the wrists or bend in the one line from the shoulder to the club face.

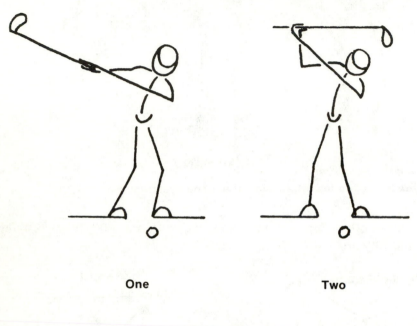

One   **Two**

Three

Figure 2.16 Lever Preferences

- Timing—The sequence of movements of the swing.

Backswing Timing

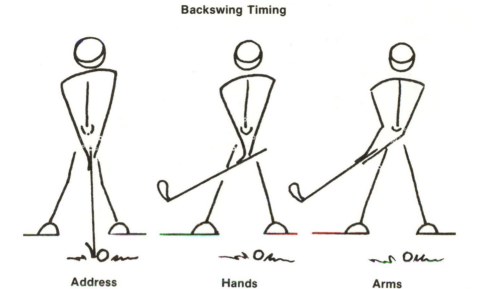

Address   Hands   Arms

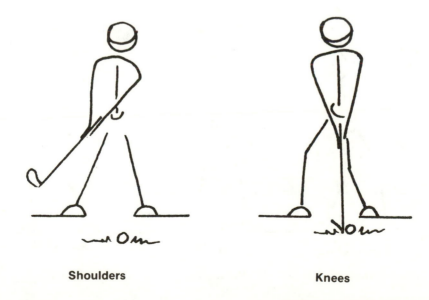

Shoulders   Knees

Figure 2.17 Timing Preferences

Forwardswing Timing

Top of Swing

Hands

Arms

Shoulders

Knees

Figure 2.18 Timing Preferences (Continued)

- Plane—The upright tilt or arc of the swing.

Individual's Ideal Plane Established with Address Posture

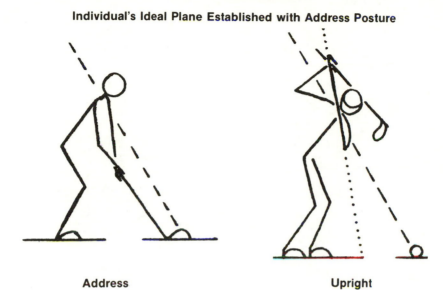

Address   Upright

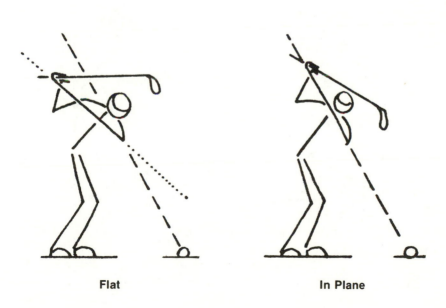

Flat   In Plane

Figure 2.19 Plane Preferences

- Release—The moment when the cocking of the wrists releases at impact forming one line from the shoulder to the clubhead.

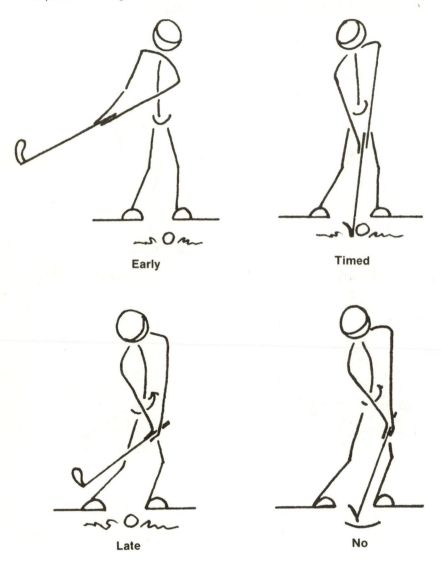

Figure 2.20 Release Preferences

- Fixed Center—A spot in space at the approximate top of the sternum that acts as the hub of the swing.

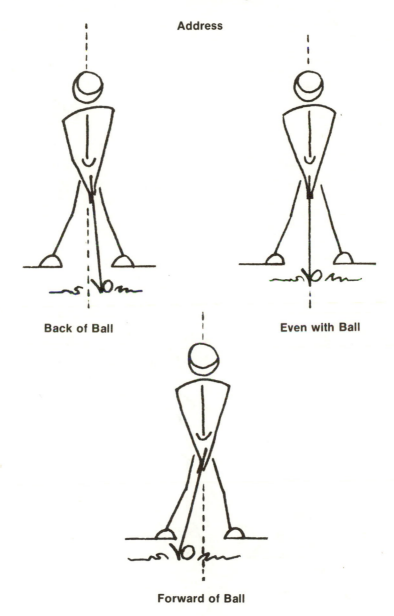

Figure 2.21 Swing Center Preferences

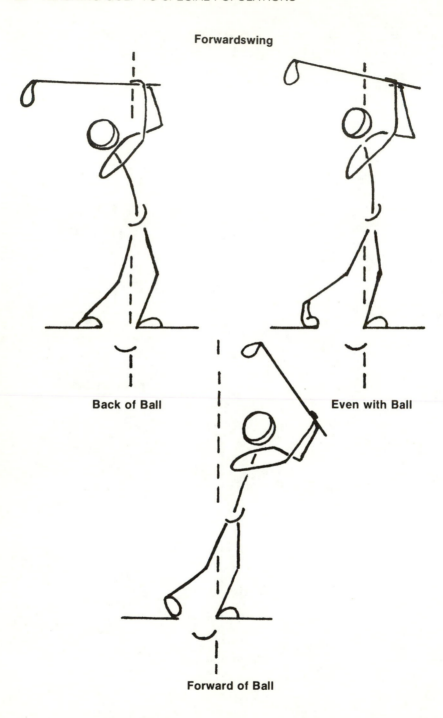

Figure 2.22 Swing Center Preferences (Continued)

Backswing

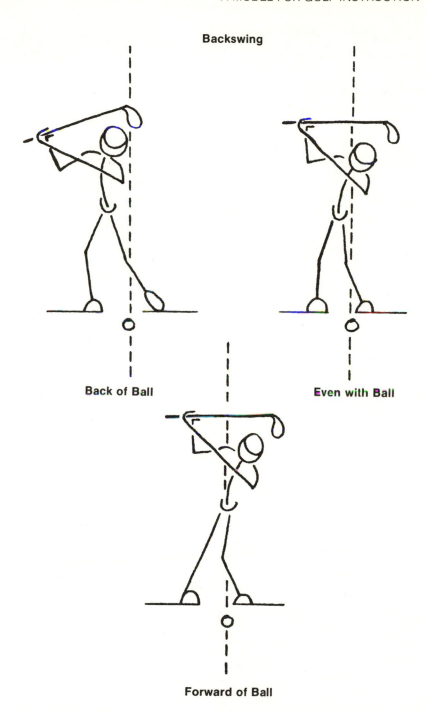

Figure 2.23 Swing Center Preferences (Continued)

• Balance—The ability to transfer the weight from the target side to the rear side and a return to the target side without losing balance.

Controlled

Falls Back

Falls Forward

Stationary

Figure 2.24 Balance Preferences

Pre-Swing Front View

- Target Hand
  - ☐ top
  - ☐ neutral
  - ☐ under
- Rear hand
  - ☐ top
  - ☐ neutral
  - ☐ under
- Ball Position
  - ☐ back of center
  - ☐ center
  - ☐ forward of center
- Stance
  - ☐ narrower than shoulders
  - ☐ shoulder width
  - ☐ wider than shoulders

In-Swing Front View

- Width of Arc at Impact
  - ☐ extended
  - ☐ collapsed
- Length of Arc
  - ☐ below parallel
  - ☐ parallel
  - ☐ short of parallel
- Position at the Top
  - ☐ cupped
  - ☐ square
  - ☐ hyperextended
- Lever
  - ☐ 1
  - ☐ 2
  - ☐ 3
- Release
  - ☐ early
  - ☐ tuned
  - ☐ late
  - ☐ no
- Dynamic Balance
  - ☐ yes, controlled
  - ☐ no, falls back
  - ☐ no, falls forward
  - ☐ no, stationary
- Posture
  - ☐ weight rear foot
  - ☐ weight even
  - ☐ weight target foot
- Backswing Timing
  - ☐ hand
  - ☐ arm
  - ☐ shoulder
  - ☐ leg

- Forwardswing Timing
  - ☐ hand
  - ☐ arm
  - ☐ shoulder
  - ☐ leg
- Address Swing Center
  - ☐ back of ball
  - ☐ even with ball
  - ☐ forward of ball
- Backswing Swing Center
  - ☐ back of ball
  - ☐ even with ball
  - ☐ forward of ball
- Forwardswing Swing Center
  - ☐ back of ball
  - ☐ even with ball
  - ☐ forward of ball

Pre-Swing Down The Line View

- Blade Alignment
  - ☐ open
  - ☐ square
  - ☐ closed
- Feet Alignment
  - ☐ open
  - ☐ square
  - ☐ closed
- Hip Alignment
  - ☐ open
  - ☐ square
  - ☐ closed
- Shoulder Alignment
  - ☐ open
  - ☐ square
  - ☐ closed
- Heel-Toe Weight Distribution
  - ☐ weight on heels
  - ☐ weight even
  - ☐ weight forward
- Body Inclination At Address
  - ☐ sitting back
  - ☐ over ball
  - ☐ standing tall

In-Swing Down The Line View

- Plane
  - ☐ upright
  - ☐ in plane
  - ☐ flat

Table 2.1 Checklist for Swing Evaluation

A checklist for use in evaluating the golf swing which incorporates the principles and preferences is provided in Table 2.1. For an instructor the checklist is a convenient way to help the student understand his swing. In addition the visual reinforcer helps the instructor become more aware of potential preference alignments for swing efficiency.

With all of the modern research tools available to us today, we are better able to understand the simplest way to help individuals combine preferences to produce the most efficient swing for them. Special adaptations in preferences will have to be made in order to accommodate various special problems that occur with the wide variety of handicaps. In order for the adaptations to be understood and used, Chapter 4 provides an outline of a standard or model for the basic full swing, short shot and putting.

CHAPTER 3

Evolution Of The Modern Golf Swing

by DeDe Owens

Golf is a game of adaptation. Each golfer must learn to adapt to the specific nature and characteristics of the environment—the length of the hole, width of the fairway, weather conditions, etc.

Historically, the golf swing has undergone a number of changes based on environmental requirements. The changes have greatly influenced the swing styles observed today. As golf instructors, we must not only understand what influenced the development of the golf swing, but also what swing styles have resulted.

Each golfer, whether handicapped or not, must also be prepared to adapt his or her game. Each individual's size, shape, strength, etc., influences his swing characteristics. In special populations this merely requires a more careful analysis of the individual's capacities.

The following chapter presents a condensed evolution of the modern golf swing. The evolution will be discussed from two perspectives. The first is an isolation of significant influences which have guided and altered the swing through the years. The second is a comparative approach implementing the principles and preferences aspects of Wiren's model presented in the previous chapters. The swing will be described with respect to three styles, or collective swing characteristics, representative of specific eras in the evolution of the modern golf swing: The classical, classical-modern, and modern swing styles.

Significant Influences

The exact origin of golf is unknown, but the game as it is played today, with 18 holes, was founded at St. Andrews Golf Course in Scotland around 1744. The location and physical description of St. Andrews is not unlike other Scottish courses of that day. An appreciation of these conditions enhances the understanding of the overall development of the golf swing.

The St. Andrews Golf Course, due to a limited amount of arable land, was laid out between sand dunes. This land had been used for sheep grazing. It was, and is today, a "links course" (seaside) open and fairly unprotected except for the dunes, and subjected to the cold and sometimes harsh prevailing winds off the sea. The climatic conditions directly influence the dress of the golfers by requiring heavier protective clothing to shield against the wind and cold. In addition, the sparseness of grass plus the drying effect of the winds produced hard, flat fairways. As a result, the golf swing that developed was influenced by

- restrictive clothing
- the need for stability in playing in the wind
- the desire to produce a ball flight trajectory low enough to be controlled in the wind while simultaneously maximizing the roll provided by the hard ground to gain distance.

As the game of golf became more popular, it spread to the United States with its variable terrain and climatic conditions. Golfers were no longer constantly plagued by high winds. A milder climate predominated, and the terrain was rolling and grassy. With these differences, the game as it was played in Scotland was not applicable. There was a need to hit higher or more lofted shots because of the terrain and lack of roll that contributed to distance. Similarly, the less restrictive dress also allowed the swing to become freer and take on a different appearance than its Scottish predecessor.

The evolution of the modern swing was also influenced by the equipment. The clubs used in the later 1800's and early 1900's were wooden shafted and made primarily of hickory or apple wood. Wooden shafts have particular characteristics which differ from the steel shafts of today (developed around 1929). The first is the torqueing action in which wooden shafts turn or twist, causing the face to open and close. Steel has less torque with more of a lateral bend as opposed to a turning or twisting action. The second major distinction is in the whippiness or flexibility of the shafts. Wooden shafts are softer and give more easily than steel.

Wooden shafts were handmade, and therefore varied from club to club, based on the type and age of the wood. Today machines gauge the flexibility of a shaft, whereas the sensitivity of the player's hands determined the club choice of wooden shafts. Today the flex of a club (desired degree of flexibility) can be artificially produced through the placement of flex patterns in the shaft of the club.

The amount of torque, combined with the flexibility of the wooden shaft, produced swings which necessitated more hand action characterized by a "pushing action" from the rear side. This hand action was required in order to "time" the impact position. Without active hands while using wooden shafts, the club would trail the hands in the swing, producing a variety of ball flight patterns. Steel shafted clubs require less hand action and manipulation. The swings with steel shafts developed into more powerful "hitting" actions. In contrast, the motion used in swinging the wooden shafts was more rhythmical and flowing. Steel shafts thus produced a significant change in the evolution of the modern golf swing.

An additional influence was the role of competition, communication and observation. It was not until inter-city competitions and later organized tournaments that the improvements in the golf swing began to emerge. Initially, the style of the best golfer in a particular locality was copied. Therefore, each individual golfer could be identified by his or her characteristic style as being from a particular area or influenced by a local player's style. Association, imitation and experimentation provided the impetus for many swing improvements. No doubt many individual styles existed and were tried. However, only those that produced the desired and consistent results prevailed.

The use of photographic techniques also influenced the communication and imitation of swing styles and the analysis of the golf techniques of leading players. As early as 1899, instructors were suggesting that beginners in the game study the "instantaneous" photographs of leading players to understand and learn the game. Today cameras of all descriptions are used (still, sequence cameras, 16mm and 8mm movie cameras, video cameras, etc.) in the analysis of the golf swing.

The influence of the mass media on communication cannot be overlooked in spreading the popularity of golf. Since the mid-1830's (and possibly earlier) sports journalists have expanded public knowledge of and exposure to golf and other sports. The direct effect of modern television and the sophisticated techniques in television with simultaneous angle shots and instant replay on the interest in golf and swing analysis cannot be measured.

The swing action of the three styles may be described in terms of two force producing motions, pulling and/or pushing. To illustrate, a right-handed golfer has his left side closest to the target (target side) and his right side away from the target (rear side). Using target and rear side, if an individual exhibits a throwing (or pushing) action, the swing motion is from the rear side, and thus referred to as "rear side dominance." If on the other hand, the individual exhibits a pulling action in which the swing force is leading or in front of the ball, this represents a "target side dominant" swing. The continuum presented in Figure 3.1 depicts the evolution of the three golf swing in terms of the type of swing force produced.

The evolution of the modern golf swing (i.e., the swing style of Jack Nicklaus) included a transitional period in which the swing characteristics changed from rear side dominance (classical) to target side dominance (modern). It is, however, important to recognize that these changes in swing also reflect the changes in equipment

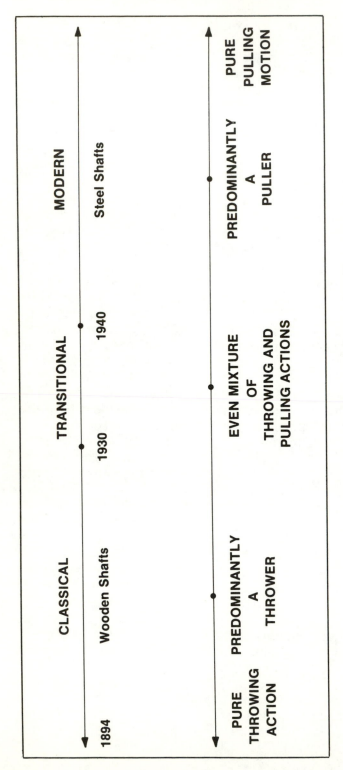

Figure 3.1   Timeline of the Evolution of the Modern Golf Swing and
Corresponding Characteristics of the Force Produced
(Adapted from Flick, 1972)

(wooden to steel shafts), climate (cold and windy to mild), terrain (flat to hilly) and apparel (restricted to free). The golf swing characteristics, therefore, reflect a variety of physical, cultural and environmental influences.

An understanding of the types of swings and the factors influencing them is important. Each style (classical, classical-modern and modern) has particular swing characteristics, some very similar and some very different from the other styles. For example, the wooden shafted clubs required considerable wrist action early in the downswing phase to be effective. Therefore, active hands were efficient. With steel shafts, less wrist action early in the swing is required. Too much wrist action, too early in the swing, is less efficient with steel shafts. It would be noted that the terms "efficient" and "less efficient" are used rather than "correct or incorrect," "right or wrong," "good or bad." There is no value judgment implied.

All three swing styles are used today. All three are effective. The important element in which ever style utilized is the understanding of the characteristics of each swing. The effects of intermingling swing characteristics may produce less efficient swing actions than desired.

The following section presents a historical perspective of the evolution of the modern golf swing. A description of each swing style is provided. A summary of the swing characteristic of the three styles is presented with pictures representative of the swing styles. These are included for evaluation and comparison.

Classical Swing—The classical swing is characterized by a throwing action (rear side dominant) in which the hands and arms supply the power. The body sways as the weight moves from the target side to rear side on the backswing with the arms following the body. The position at the top of swing is one of loose hands with the grip held between the thumb and first two fingers. The target arm is bent and the rear arm is behind and away from the body. The club position is below parallel. The downswing is initiated and dominated by a slashing action of the arms and hands with the upper body following the arms. The club is released early in the downswing to allow the clubhead to catch up with the hands at impact. The upper body at the finish of the swing is forward of the target foot, with the arms around to the target side and below the shoulder, the result of a flat arc back and through the ball.

The physical appearance and attire pictured in Figure 3.2 is representative of the day. The restricted appearance of the swing is in part a function of the clothing. In addition, the restrictiveness reflects a hand dominated swing which results in a lifting, loose swing. This may be contrasted with what will be seen in the modern swing (Figure 6.4) as a stretched or extended appearance. The stretched appear-

Table 3.1 Summary of Preferences Demonstrated by Classical, Classical-Modern, and Modern Swing Styles

Principles	Styles		
	Classical	Classical-Modern	Modern
		Preferences	
Grip			
• Left hand (target hand)	3 to 4 knuckles	2 to 3 knuckles	1 to 2 knuckles
• Right hand (rear hand)	no knuckles	1 to 2 knuckles	1 to 2 knuckles
Set-up			
• Ball Position	center of stance	center to forward	forward of center
• Stance	wider than shoulder	shoulder width	shoulder width
• Alignment			
Feet	closed	square	slightly open
Hips	closed	square to slightly closed	square
Shoulders	closed	square to slightly closed	square
Blade	open	square to slightly closed	square
Length of Arc	below	short of parallel to parallel	parallel
Position at Top	cupped	cupped	square
Lever	3	2	2
Width of Arc	collapsed	extended	extended
Release	early	early to timed	timed
Dynamic Balance	yes/no	yes	yes

Posture	yes/no	yes	yes
• Lateral Weight Distribution	heels	even	even
• Heel-Toe Weight Distribution	heels	even	balls of feet
• Angular Body Position	standing tall	over to tall	over ball
Timing			
• Backswing	shoulders	arms	hands
• Forwardswing	hands	hip to knees	knees
Swing Center			
• Address	even with ball	even with ball	back of ball
• Backswing	back of ball	even with ball	back of ball
• Forwardswing	ahead of ball	even with ball	even with ball
Plane	flat	flat to in plane	in plane to upright

Address   Top of Swing   Follow-through

CLASSICAL

CLASSICAL-MODERN

MODERN

**Figure 3.2 Collective View of the Three Swing Styles.
(Courtesy PGA, Hermanson, 1972)**

ance is a result of an arm swing. The hand oriented swing is a function also of the equipment (wooden shafts) which required manipulation to achieve the desired results at impact. The steel shafts required less and were more applicable for the arm swing of the modern swing.

Classical-Modern Swing—The majority of players today have swing styles that would be classified as classical-modern. This style combines characteristics of the classical and modern golf swings. For the average player, the classical-modern swing is "easier," requiring less effort. The classical characteristics described previously include rhythm, body rotation or turn, weight transfer from an even weight distribution at address to the rear from the target foot, cupped hand position at the top and some degree of active hands. The modern characteristics are a forward ball position, arm swing, two levers, a rear parallel swing arc, extended position at impact and more leg action. The classical-modern player is not a pure thrower or pure puller but possesses characteristics of each, some to a greater or lesser degree than others. However, due to equipment advances (wooden to steel shafts) an individual would not be a pure thrower and be effective with steel shafts, nor a puller with wooden shafts. The classical-modern swing blends the naturalness and free flowing motion of the classical swing with the power positions of the more contrived, tension producing modern swing.

Modern Swing—The modern swing, in contrast to the classical swing, is characterized by a pulling action (target side dominance) in which the lower body leads the upper body. The proper sequential action would allow for the latest possible release of the clubhead to impart the maximum force at impact. In the backswing the lower body provides a resistance for the coiling of the upper body around a center of rotation with minimum hip turn and a full shoulder turn. The initial address position with more bend of the upper body from the top of the thighs allows the club to be swung back in a longer and more upright arc. The target hand at the top of the swing is flat and the club is parallel to the ground. The forwardswing is initiated prior to the full completion of the backswing by a lateral move of the knees toward the target. This in effect establishes the pulling action and dominance of the target side. The upper body follows with the arms and hands coming last in the sequence.

In appreciating the evolution it should be noted that no value judgment has been, or should be, placed on any of the three swing styles. The most important aspect of a golf swing, whether classical, classical-modern, or modern, is its efficiency and the ability of an individual to execute the style most appropriate for his or her capabilities and limitations. This is a very important aspect when working with all golfers and most certainly with the handicapped.

A summary of the swing styles is presented in Table 3.1 with pictures characteristic of each respective style in Figure 3.2. From Table 3.1 it can be seen that there are similarities and differences between the swing styles. However, within each style the interaction of the preferences are non-contradictory.

References

Dobereiner, P. *The Glorious World of Golf.* New York: McGraw-Hill, 1973.

Flick, J.M. "The Modern Swing." In *Teaching Methods.* Edited by R. Hermanson. Professional Golfers Association of America, 1972.

Hermanson, R. *Teaching Methods.* Professional Golfers Association of America, 1972.

Hutchinson, H.G. *The Book of Golf and Golfers.* London: Longmans, Green and Co., 1899.

Revell, A.H. *The Pro and Con of Golf.* Chicago: Rand-McNally and Company, 1915.

Tolhurst, D. "Is the 'Modern Swing' Wrecking Your Game?" *Golf Magazine* (April, 1977): 50-56.

Webster's Dictionary. Springfield: G.C. Merriam Company, 1977.

Wiren, G. *The Search for the Perfect Teaching Method.* National Golf Foundation Information Sheet. 1976, ES-7, 1-5

CHAPTER 4

Techniques Of Golf Instruction: Full Swing

by Carol Johnson and Ann Johnstone

The full swing is used when maximum distance is desired for a given club. The principles and preferences used for the FULL swing are as follows:

Grip—A good grip is very essential to a good golf swing. Hands which are efficiently placed on the golf club will lead to excellent club face control. There are three commonly used grips: ten finger, overlapping, and interlocking. The three grips are almost the same except the position of the little finger on the rear hand changes.

- Target Hand—The back of the hand is facing the target, with one knuckle to two knuckles showing, but rarely three or four. The club is placed diagonally across the palm with the "V" formed by the index finger and thumb pointing to a spot between the chin and rear shoulder.
- Rear Hand—The palm of the rear hand is facing the target. The life line will cover the target side thumb. The "V" formed by the index finger and the thumb should point to a spot between the chin and rear shoulder. One to two knuckles are showing, but very rarely three or four.

When using the ten finger grip, all the fingers are on the club with no overlapping of fingers. For the overlapping grip the little finger of the rear hand overlaps the index finger of the target hand. When the interlocking grip is used, the rear hand little finger and the index finger of the target hand interlock. The pressure used for the full swing is modest but not stifling; firm pressure but not taut.

Aim

- Club Face Alignment—The club face is square to the target line with the scoring lines perpendicular to the target lines. The sole of the club is resting on the ground
- Body Alignment—The body is parallel to the target line. The feet, knees, hips, and shoulders are all parallol to the target line.

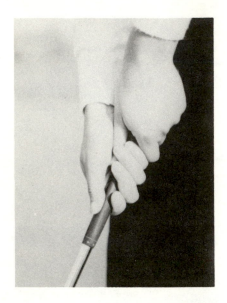 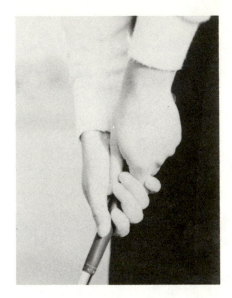

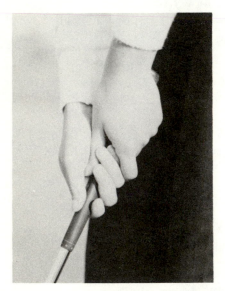

Ten finger grip (top left), interlocking grip (top right), overlapping grip (bottom).

Figure 4.1 **A good grip is essential** to a good golf swing.

Figure 4.2 **There are three types of stances.**

Square (top left), open (top right), closed (left).

Figure 4.3 Club face alingment. Correct (left), incorrect (right).

Down the line closed (top right), down the line open (top left), down the line square (left).

Figure 4.4   Club face alignment.

Set-up-Stance—There are three types of stances, the open, closed and square. The square stance is used for most of the shots in golf.
- Square Stance—The toes are parallel to the intended line of flight. Because the toes are often fanned out, it is best to check the alignment of the feet by assuring that the toe line is parallel to the target line.
- Open Stance—The target foot is slightly pulled back from its parallel position to the target line.
- Closed Stance—The rear foot is slightly pulled back from its parallel position to the target line.
- Set-up-Weight Distribution—The weight should be equally distributed on each foot with more weight toward the balls of the feet.
- Set-up-Body Posture—The body is in a general ready position or athletic posture. The trunk is bent forward at the top of the thighs. The knees are flexed and arms hang down easily from the shoulders.
- Set-up-Ball Position—The ball is placed in the stance slightly toward the target side of the center.

Radius of the Swing (Arc Width)—The radius of the swing (the length of the target arm plus the club) changes with the length of the club. The radius is the longest with the driver and the shortest with the wedge. The extended target side arm determines the length of the arc.

Position at the Top of the Back Swing—The target hand and the club face are in a square position at the top of the back swing.

Arc Length or Circumference of the Swing—For the full swing the hands are approximately shoulder high and the club is almost parallel to the ground.

Lever—The angle created by the wrist cock at the top of the back swing places the target arm in a two lever position. This position, when released at impact, creates most of the speed in the swing.

Timing—In the timing sequence of the swing, the hands are #1, the arms #2 and the hips and legs #3. On the back swing the sequence is 1,2,3 and reversing its order on the forward swing, 3,2,1.

Plane—The tilt of the circumference of the swing is the plane. Taller players have a more upright plane while the shorter players have a flatter plane.

Release—When the wrists are cocked or placed in a two lever position on the back swing, the return of the hands and arms to the starting position constitutes the desired release at impact.

Fixed Center—A point in space, approximately at the top of the sternum, acts as the hub of the swing. It should remain relatively stationary until after the hit.

Balance—The body should remain in balance as the weight transfers to the rear foot and back to the target foot for the hit.

In golf instruction, as in other sports, implementing drills and exercises to simulate the desired motions without the intimidating presence of the ball helps the students develop a free motion. It is important to note that the motion is not the exact motion as if the ball was being struck. However, it helps create an image or picture of the overall motion. The following drills and exercises can be used to teach a full swing. Additional drills can be found in the references provided.

Drills And Exercises For The Full Swing

- Towel Exercise—In the set-up position (address position), grasp a large twisted towel at each end, palm of target hand down, palm or rear hand up, and extend both arms until towel is taut. Swing arms, shoulders and body away from the target (the back to the target), then swing towards the target and finish high with belt buckle towards the target. Repeat several times, then at the top of the back swing and as you start forward, let go of the towel with the rear hand and pull the towel with the left hand only to a high finish; repeat several times.
- Timing Your Swing—Take a club in your hand and swing it slowly back and then accelerate through. Say "back and through," or "one and two"; swish the air; sing songs like "Hello Dolly." It is a feeling like Ready, Set, Go. To get a louder swish noise, hold the club in the neck part of the club (upside down), and swing it back and forth making swish sounds. Swing it back and forth using the right hand only and then the left hand only. Repeat.
- Sequence of the Swing—Number your hands, arms and hips and body—#1 hands, #2 arms, #3 hips and body. On the back swing have #1 hands start, closely followed by #2 arms and #3 hips and body. For the forward swing you reverse the numbers and start with the #3, hips and body, followed by #2 arms and #1 hands. So your sequence of swing should be 1-2-3, 3-2-1.
- Club Low Through the Hitting Area—Put a ball down, and put a tee in the ground about 6 inches in front and one about 6 inches behind the ball. As you take your back swing, try to hit the tee 6 inches behind the ball and on your forward swing try to hit the tee that is 6 inches in front of the ball. This should help to keep the club head low through the hitting area.
- "C" and "I" Position—At the address position imagine yourself in a bent position; call it an imaginary "C". Swing to the top of the back swing and remain in that imaginary "C" position. Remain a "C" through the hitting area and then finish high or into a taller posture, an imaginary "I" position.

- Hitting the Ball in "South America"—Imagine the golf ball as the World. The stripe around the center of the golf ball would be the equator, the top would be North Pole and down a bit would be North America. The bottom would be South America. Strive to hit the ball in South America and the ball will go up; if the ball is hit above the equator, the ball will go down. So strive to hit your ball in the lower half or below the equator in order to produce a higher ball flight.

CHAPTER 5

Techniques Of Golf Instruction: The Short Shot And Putting

by Carol Johnson and Ann Johnstone

Short Shot

The short shot describes those shots that are taken from within fifty yards of the green. Some shots are hit with a very low trajectory such as the five-iron would produce. Shots will loft high into the air and land softly if they have been hit with the more lofted wedge. The considerations of the lie of the ball, the distance it must travel in the air, the roll on the surface, plus weather factors and surface conditions are included in shot decision making and will be discussed more fully.

Unlike the full shot, which is used mainly for *distance,* the short shot emphasizes *direction.* Club selection affords one of the simplest ways to get a variety of height and roll on the ball. Generally, the 5, 6, 7, 8, 9 irons and wedges are used. The 5-iron produces a shot that carries about $^1/_3$ in the air and rolls approximately $^2/_3$ on the surface. The 7-iron carries about ½ in the air and rolls about ½ the distance. The wedges loft at least $^2/_3$ of the distance in the air and roll about $^1/_3$ of the distance on the green. The player must select the club that will land in the area desired.

The short shot *Principles* and basic modern *Preferences* are as follows:

- Grip—The standard basic hand relationship to the club face is used. The back of the target hand and the palm of the rear hand face the target. The hands will be moved down the shaft of the club for the shorter distances and back up to the top of the shaft for the longer shots. The pressure in the hands will be firmer on the uphill and longer shots and somewhat lighter on the downhill and shorter shots.
- Aim—The feet, hips, and shoulders are square or slightly open to the target. The club face is square or open.

- Set-up—The stance is narrow for the very short 15 yard shot and becomes only slightly wider for the 45 yard shots. There is a definite feeling of lowering the center of gravity and being "down" over the shot. For the 15 yard shots the weight may be as much as 70% on the target foot and as the shot requires more distance, the weight should be more equally distributed.
- Width of Arc—The arc is shortened by gripping down on the shaft for the 15 yard shots. The arc is lengthened to within two or three inches of the top of the club for the longer shots.
- Position of the Hands—The hands remain square to the target throughout the swing.
- Length of the Arc—The arc length varies. Imagine the player using his or her hands and arms as if they were hands on a clock. A 15 yard shot will be produced if the hands of the player swing from 7:00 to 5:00. Thirty yards will be the result of an 8:00 to 4:00 swing, and a 45 yard shot will be produced if the hands are swung from 9:00 to 3:00.
- Lever—With the clock concept, lengthening the arc produces more distance. The levering action is only necessary when the hands are in the 9:00 to 3:00 swing. The levering action produces more clubhead speed needed for the 45 yard distance. There is little or no bending of the wrists until the desired distance is over 30 yards.
- Timing—For the 7:00 to 5:00, 15 yard shot, the hands and arms work back and forth together in a triangular action with little or no leg action. For the 30 yard shot the hands, arms, and shoulders still work as a unit, and there is an easing or reacting of the legs, almost as a one piece movement.
- Plane—The plane of the short shot is more upright, with an attempt toward a straight path. The plane is very similar on the backward and forward swing.
- Release—For the 15 and 30 yard shots the triangular set of the hands and arms does not produce a levering or cocking action, therefore no release. The 45 yard length with its need for power, sets the lever at approximately waist height and it releases at impact.
- Fixed Center—There is no movement of the center.
- Balance—The short 15 yard shots have the weight and balance toward the target foot. The weight and balance transfer slightly to the rear foot and return to the target foot during the 30 yard shot. The transfer is more noticeable from the target foot to the rear foot and returned to the target foot during the 45 yard waist high shot.

Short Approach Shots

In teaching short approach shots there are a number of ball flight influences which affect the ball when it lands. These influences, plus individual ability, should be considered prior to executing the chosen shot. The choices can be viewed with respect to graduated *levels of control and difficulty* (level 1 = simplest, to level 4 = most difficult). Table 5-1 provides a summary of the four levels. The similarities and differences between the levels and the standard short shot model provided in this chapter are presented. The progression from level 1 to level 4 requires modifications in the application of the Laws and Principles. These modifications allow for control in the trajectory and therefore softness of the ball on landing. For example, the higher the trajectory of the ball, the less it will roll on landing. However, this ball flight trajectory is more difficult to produce than a lower trajectory (Table 5.1).

From an instructional view it is important to understand the concept of levels. However, the vast majority of our students may never execute beyond the level one shot (simplest). If the major objective of all approach shots (i.e. all levels) is to get the ball on the green, then the major distinction between the levels is "how close" to the pin. "How close" necessitates that the golfer assess two conditions: the requirements of the shot, and his ability to execute the shot.

The first condition, the requirements of the shot, has three considerations (LTD): the lie of the ball; the trajectory desired; and the distance required. The better the lie of the ball, the more shot selections are possible. The tighter the lie, the fewer options are available. Based on the lie of the ball, the desired shot is selected with regard to the situation. For example: are there bunkers between the ball and the green, is the area relatively open, flat and/or hilly, and how much green is there to work with before and after the pin? With these questions answered and the shot selected, the amount of swing motion (i.e. swing arc length and speed) is determined for the given distance.

With some guidance, the majority of golfers can assess the requirements of the shot. However, the greatest failing of golfers is their assessment of shot selection relative to their ability to execute. Regardless of the ability of the golfer, beginner to advanced, the shot selection, or plan of action should be based on percentages. That is, which shot, given the situation, is the one which can be most often and most effectively executed with a high degree of success? Obviously, the golfer with the greater skill will have more level options available because he has more control of the swing.

If we take typical approach shot situations into a green, the variations which are possible will provide a better understanding for the four levels. Note that as the levels progress from 1 to 4, the amount of control and degree of difficulty increases because of the modifications in the laws and principles to produce a higher, softer shot landing on the green.

Table 5.1
Preference Summary of the Approach Shot Levels

	Level One	Level Two	Level Three	Level Four
Percentage of Shots	**80%**	**10%**	**5%**	**5%**
Club Selection	9-iron, pitching or sand wedge	pitching or wedge	same level two	same level two
Laws				
• Speed	good form lively speed	very slow and sustained (greatest effect on shot)	same level one	same level two
• Path	square to target line	same level one	left	same level three
• Face	square to target line	same level one	open	same level three
• Angle of Approach	upswing	same level one	same level one	same level one
Principles				
• Grip	standard	standard with lighter grip pressure	same level one	same level two
• Aim	square shoulders slightly open feet and hips	standard	open (all)	same level three
• Set-up	a. feet fairly close	a. feet wider than level one	same level one	same level one
	b. ball position forward	b. ball position same level one		
	c. weight favors target foot	c. weight even both feet		

Table 5.1 (continued)
Preference Summary of the Approach Shot Levels

	Level One	Level Two	Level Three	Level Four
● Width of Arc	grip club within 2-3" from the top	grip club 1-2" from the top	same level two	grip club 2" from top
● Hand Position	standard	standard	standard	standard
● Length of Arc	8:00 to 4:00	10:00 to 2:00	9:00 to 3:00	10/11:00 to 1/2:00
● Lever	one	two	same level two	same level two
● Timing	standard	same level one	same level one	same level one
● Release	none	at impact	same level two	same level two
● Fixed Center	even with ball at address and maintained	same level one	same level one	same level one
● Balance	weight transfers as a reaction to the shot	weight transfers	same level two	same level two (resembles full swing)
Skill Level Necessary for Execution	Beginner-Advanced	Intermediate to Advanced	Advanced	Advanced

Situation A

The player is faced with a good lie in which he is 30 yards from the green. The ball must travel over a bunker 20 yards in front of the ball. The pin is 10 yards from the fringe of the green. The green is 30 yards long.

Requirements of the Shot
- Lie - good/ sitting up
- Trajectory - medium
- Distance - depends on shot selection

Shot Selection

Options Available	Ability	% Selection	Club Selection
All	Beginner	level 1	9-iron
(Standard-level 4)	Intermediate	level 1	9-iron
	Advanced	level 1	9-iron

Logic for Selection

The conditions of the situation do not require trajectory or roll control beyond that possible with the standard level one shot. The 10 yards in front of the pin and 20 yards beyond allow for adequate shot control. Level one therefore is the highest percentage shot for all abilities to (1) get the ball on the green and (2) get close to the pin.

Situation B

The player is faced with the same conditions as in situation A except for the lie, which is tight.

Requirements of the Shot
- Lie - bad/ tight
- Trajectory - medium
- Distance - depends on shot selection

Shot Selection

Options Available	Ability	% Selection	Club Selection
Standard-level 2	beginner	standard	P.W.
	Intermediate	standard (1)	P.W.
	Advanced	standard (1)	P.W.

Logic for Selection

When the lie becomes tighter, it creates the need for a more descending or steeper angle of approach. This is accommodated by a ball position which is center to slightly back of center in the stance. This is the positioning for the standard model (Chapter 4), therefore no adaptations are necessary. The club selection, pitching wedge, provides the additional trajectory with the standard swing. Adjusting the ball position slightly, the intermediate and advanced players retain a high percentage in executing the level one shot.

Situation C

The player is faced with the same conditions as Situation A except the pin is 5 yards from the fringe of the green.

Requirements of the Shot

- Lie - good
- Trajectory - high
- Distance - depends on shot selection

Shot Selection

Options Available	Ability	% Selection	Club Selection
level 1-level 4	Beginner	level 2	P.W.
	Intermediate	level 2	P.W.
	Advanced	level 2,3	S.W.

Logic for Selection

The change in shot requirements to a higher trajectory creates the need for a level two shot. This variation incorporates a longer back swing and a slower swing speed forward which makes it more difficult than level one. However, it can be accomplished by most golfers if the need arises.

The advanced player is capable of using a level three shot in this situation. It is more complex with changes in stance, swing path and the face of the club at impact. These adaptations produce a higher trajectory than a level two shot and a much softer landing. Difficulty often arises when not enough swing motion is allowed for the added height and resulting decrease in distance.

(**Note:** When the pin placements become tighter the margin for error decreases. Accordingly the complexity of the shot selection should decrease depending upon skill ability. The objective on the approach may change from getting close to the pin to getting safely on the green.)

Situation D

The player is faced with a situation where the ball is either sitting behind a tree or in a bunker with a steep lip. The distance to the pin is 10 to 15 yards and a short target area.

Requirements of the Shot

- Lie - good
- Trajectory - very high
- Swing motion - depends on shot selection

Shot Selection

Options Available	Ability	% Selection	Club Selection
level 1-level 4	Beginner	level 1,2	P.W.
	Intermediate	level 2,3	P.W./S.W.
	Advanced	level 4	P.W./S.W.

Logic for Selection

The shot requirement of a very high trajectory to a small landing area from a difficult position necessitates a level four shot. Level four requires four major changes from the standard model in the laws with corresponding changes in the principles. The speed of the swing is very slow and sustained. The path is left. The face is open to the target and path lines, and the angle of approach is steeper. Level four should only be played by advanced golfers.

The beginner and intermediate player should choose the less complex shots. Their major objective should be to get the ball into play. That is, if the lip is too steep or the tree too high, the less direct approach is suggested. Shoot for the widest part of the green or get the ball into the fairway and then play percentages approach to the green.

Creating situations, as those presented, for our students will help them improve their understanding of shot requirements and their ability to execute. Experimentation is critical in teaching and learning. However, guidelines should be provided for some means of objective evaluation of (1) their performance (i.e. their ability to execute the four levels with x% of consistency) and (2) the situations requiring the specific levels (i.e. selecting the level based on the shot requirements and ability to execute).

Drills And Exercises For The Short Shot

- Short Swing Drill—Place a club on the ground pointing towards the target. Get into an address position, then clap your hands together and hold the club, forming a triangle with your left arm, right arm, and shoulder line. Now swing the triangle along the club back and forth. Hold the finish position and check to see if the back of the target hand is facing the target. Repeat several times.
- Club Track Drills—Place two clubs on the ground about 6 inches apart on the target line. Swing between them using your short approach shot club, 5, 6, 7, 8, 9, or wedge. This helps visualize the hitting area and hitting to a target.
- Clock Drill—Visualize a clock with your head at 12 o'clock and the ball at 6 o'clock. Hit some shots keeping your parts equal on the backswing and forward swing. Example 7 o'clock to 5 o'clock, 8 o'clock to 4 o'clock, 9 o'clock to 3 o'clock.
- Spot Practicing—Hit toward general areas, then specific areas, and then on exact spots. Put a dime on the green and aim at that dime; when you hit the dime, move it around so you will have different spots at which to aim.
- Visualize the Shots—Visualize the shot you want to perform; then take the correct club and hit the shot. If you want the ball to go 1/3

Figure 5.1   Body posture for putting.

Figure 5.2   Ball position for putting.

in the air and run $^2/_3$, hit with a lower number club like a 5 iron. If you want the ball to go $^2/_3$ in the air and run $^1/_3$, use a 9 iron or wedge. Practice with different clubs to see the trajectory of the ball.

- One Hand Hitting—Practice hitting balls with your left hand only, then with your right hand only. Then put both hands on the club. Repeat.

Putting

One of the most important and stroke-consuming parts of the game is putting. Putters offer a great variety of styles and feel for the golfer. The different designs produce a wide assortment of feel which can be changed to accommodate different putting surfaces. Because the hands of the players have such different needs for feel, putting is so individualized that the combination of workable preferences is unlimited.

The following putting principles and preferences suggest some of the successful, commonly used preferences.

Grip—Use the standard ten finger, overlapping or interlocking grips. The hands are generally more relaxed with the thumbs straight down the center of the grip. Common variations are described below.

- Reverse Overlap—The rear hand is placed on the club with the target hand index finger overlapping the little finger of the rear hand. Some players overlap one or more fingers of the target hand over the rear fingers.
- Cross Handed Putting—In cross handed putting, the rear hand is placed at the top of the club with the target hand below it. For this form of putting the hands are sometimes separated on the grip of the putter. The pressure of the grip is modest with more firmness used on longer or uphill putts and a softer, more gentle pressure on the downhill and shorter putts.

Aim—A good alignment has the stance, club face, body, hands, and shoulders square to the target line.

Set-up—A squared stance, open or closed, may be used.

- Body Posture—There is, generally, a more bent over posture. The bend from the hips is more exaggerated until the eyes are directly over or slightly behind the ball or the target line. The center of gravity is lowered, with the knees slightly flexed.
- Ball Position—The ball is placed in the stance from a mid-point between the feet to a position as far forward as a position off the target foot.
- Width of the Stance—Both the width of the stance and the placement of the weight vary greatly. An important objective is that the body is in good balance with enough stability to keep motionless during the stroke.

Arc Width—A short radius is more common than a very upright long arc. The club lengths vary from the different club designs and shaft lengths, but the body bend usually produces a shorter width to the arc.

Position—The hands remain square to the target throughout.

Arc Length—Maximum control is obtained because the back swing and the forward swing are kept very short.

Lever—There is very little levering action in most putting strokes. There are some players who have more wristy preference for putting and their style has a bit more lever.

Timing—When putting, the timing is generally slow during the back swing with acceleration through the putt. The hands, arms, and shoulders move as one unit with little or no body movement.

Plane—The plane is very upright and varies little during the swing.

Release—The putt is a one piece move. There are three general types of strokes. All except the wristy putt have very little noticeable release.

• Stroke Putt—The back swing and follow through are of equal length. A one foot back swing has about a one foot follow through.
• Wristy Putt—The wrist bend or breaking of the wrists on the putt of this kind is a variation from the cocking of the full swing. Wrist putting uses a flexing and extending action—forward and backward with both wrists using the same action.
• Tap Putt—A short back swing and a tapping action at the ball which does not follow through but stops at the ball produces the tap putt.

Fixed Center—During a putt the head and body remain steady.

Balance—There is no weight shift on a putt. Some players prefer to have the weight mainly on their target foot with the ball played off a position in front of the target toe. There are other players who place the weight equally on each foot, well-balanced between the heels and toes. With so many variables it is important to establish a firm, unmoving balance throughout the putt.

Drills And Exercises For Putting

• Putting Track Drill—Place two clubs on the putting green about 6 inches apart pointing towards the hole. Now practice your putting stroke by keeping the putter head within the track. This helps to visualize the putting line and the stroke line. Instead of using clubs for your track, use two 2 by 4's as it will be more dramatic.
• Eyes over the Ball—When addressing the ball, your eyes should be directly over the ball. Get into your putting position; take your putter to the bridge of your nose and then lower it to the ball to see if your eyes are directly over the ball. Another way to do this is take your putting position and have an extra ball in your hand; put it at the bridge of your nose and drop it—if the ball hits the one on the ground your eyes are over the ball correctly.

Some place weight equally on each foot.

Others prefer weight on target foot.

Figure 5.3   Balance.

- Yardstick Drill—Practice your putting over a yardstick. One rule of thumb would be to take the putter back one inch for every foot you have the ball go forward. Two inches for a two footer. Using a yardstick helps in seeing an inch and a foot on the putting surface.
- Tee Drill—Place a tee one foot from the hole, then two feet, then three feet from the hole, etc., until you have used ten tees and are back about ten feet. Then take three balls and start at the first one foot tee and sink the three balls. Then move back to the two foot tee, three foot tee, until you have made all three balls from each tee. If you miss one then you start all over, thus practicing your putts.
- Putting on a Rug—While away from the golf course you can practice your putting on a rug at home or in a motel room. Use the base board over floor boards to make sure your stroke is straight back and straight forward.
- Different Grip Drill—Try different type grips for putting. Use your regular golf grip to putt with, use cross handed putting, separate your hand on the grip of the club and putt. Use a reverse overlapping grip to putt with; putt with the right hand only, then putt with the left hand only. You may find a new way to hold the putter, your own personal style.

*References**

Abbott, L.; Griffin, E.; and Spork, S. *Golf Instructors' Guide*. Palm Beach: National Golf Foundation, 1980.

Gordon, R., ed. *Golf Coaches' Guide*. Palm Beach: National Golf Foundation, 1980.

Johnson, C. and Johnstone, A. *Golf: A Positive Approach*. Reading, Maine: Addison and Wesley, 1975.

Wiren, G. *The Search for a Perfect Teaching Method*. National Golf Foundation Information Sheet. 1976, 25-7, 1-5.

*References for Chapters 4 and 5.

PART 3

Teaching Golf To Individuals With Handicapping Conditions

CHAPTER 6

Assessing Present Skills And Capabilities

by DeDe Owens

Instructors who teach new students must have access to all pertinent supplementary information about each golfer in order to be most effective. When teaching special populations, your intitial assessment of each golfer is very critical. It provides an opportunity to know each person in order to create a conducive learning environment for that particular student. In addition, it provides a frame of reference for the establishment of an instructional format to best meet the needs of the student. An assessment for special populations should generally be formulated around three major areas:
- the nature of the disability
- capabilities and limitations of the individual
- personal desires and goals related to playing golf.

This chapter discusses the rationale for assessment within the three areas. Suggested topics for assessment in each area follow. The topics will be presented with an explanation for their inclusion in assessment. These are merely guidelines and are by no means intended to be restrictive. It is hoped you will be able to take these guidelines and formulate your own approaches to assessment based on your own style and method of teaching. An example of an assessment form is provided in Table 6.1.

Nature Of Disability

It is important for you as an instructor to be aware of the movement potential, capabilities and limitations of each person with whom you are working. It is not imperative that you understand the complete background of every disability, but it is important that you understand the characteristics of a given handicapping condition as they relate to the health of the golfer, and as they may provide insight and create interest in the students with whom you are working.

Table 6.1
ASSESSMENT

Name: _____ Age_____ Skill: Beg___ Int___ Adv___

Address_____ Phone_____ USGA Hd_____

A. Nature of Disability _____
    1. Type of Disability _____

    2. Medical Supervision: Yes___ No___

    If Yes: Doctor/Therapist _____ Phone_____

             Medication: Yes___ No___

             Clearance: Yes___ No___

             Restrictions: _____

             _____

B. Capabilities and Limitations

    1. Age of Onset:_____

    2. Previous Experience (Sports): _____

    _____

    3. Previous Golf Experience:_____

    4. Previous Golf Experience: Positive___ Negative___

    Explain if Negative:_____

    _____

    _____

C. Personal Desires

    1. Why do you want to play golf? _____

    _____

    2. What are your expectations? _____

    _____

    3. What are your goals in golf? _____

    _____

Type Of Disability

Disability assessment involves seeking information pertinent to movement potential in order to establish a frame of reference for instruction and perhaps adaptations and modifications in technique and/or equipment. Each student, however, must be viewed separately in order to optimize their potential as golfers, and prevent the tendency to stereotype.

Information about specific disabilities enables the teacher to determine the instructional approach and means of communication which may be for the students. A few examples may help illustrate this point:

- There are differences in working with upper and lower limb amputees with regard to balance and how you help them learn a full swing;
- There are also differences in working with blind or deaf golfers since you must learn ways to communicate directions.

Medical Supervision

It is important to know if a student of golf is under medical supervision. If so, the student should be encouraged to seek medical clearance. Consideration may be given to having the attending physician/therapist review an outline of the instructional program. In addition, many professionals in the medical field are unfamiliar with the golf swing and the movement patterns involving the twisting and acceleration of various parts. Involving medical professionals may enhance the student's feeling of support as well as create medical endorsement for future programs.

The specific motions of various body parts within the swing and the degree of intensity with which many individuals practice and play (competitive stress) may be important. To many in the medical field, golf is a sedentary sport. To the participants, it is far from sedentary, and an awareness of the skill requirements may need to be raised in both parties. For example:

- A student with chronic arthritis should avoid excessive practice when severe swelling is evident.
- A student with a history of lower back pain should avoid excessive twisting while standing flatfooted.
- An amputee with a new prosthesis must be alert for stump swelling if practice time is carried to an extreme.

Capabilities And Limitations Of Movement

Capabilities and limitations of movement in the golf swing center on range of motion, ability to bear weight on various joints, balance and weight transfer. With these considerations in mind, adaptations in swing motion and/or equipment may need to be considered.

Information about the capabilities of each student is especially pertinent, particularly to those who work with the physically disabled. The visually and hearing disabled performer should have "normal" movement potential unless his individual disability is complicated by a physical disability as well. For example:

- The motion potential of above the knee (A/K) amputees is less than that of below the knee (B/K) amputees.
- Grip modifications for arthritic hands are implemented by increasing the size of the grip (adding extra tape to the grip).
- Prosthetic adaptations are available to enhance motion during the swing for amputees.

Age of Onset of Disability

The age at which an individual became disabled will provide information relative to the development of movement patterns. Depending on the age of onset, movement potential may be enhanced, retarded or unaffected relative to that normally expected for a given maturational level. In dealing with the age of onset movement must also be viewed with respect to adaptability. If the individual is disabled early in life, he learns to adapt for movement patterns which may have been retarded or restricted. An individual disabled later in life may have an easier or harder adjustment to various movement patterns. This relates primarily to the transfer of movement concepts. Re-learning skills could present negative transfer due to inhibition. Much depends on the movements involved and the individual. For example:

- A child, blind at birth, will have more delays in motor development than those evidenced in a child blinded at five years.
- An individual who is physically disabled at 35 years has more "normal" past experiences, compared to someone disabled at 10 years.

Previous Experience

Students bring with them a variety of experiences. Some of their experiences are very limited while others are quite extensive. The information pertaining to the student's previous experiences enables the instructor to establish a line of communication. This line of communication may be one in which the backlog of experiences is drawn upon and used as building blocks for the ensuing golf experience. Many experiences will transfer in a positive manner with respect to similarities in the concepts of motion and strategies. Others may be negative in terms of motion concepts, but may become positive by providing contrasting comparisons, thereby enhancing a better understanding of swing concepts and motions. For example, contrast the wrist action in badminton, which is more of a hinging motion, to the wrist action in the golf swing which is more of a rotation.

The background information about each student golfer is pertinent to understanding the impact of past experiences on the student. Were these past contacts with golf positive or negative? The receptiveness of students to a learning situation, new or otherwise, could be directly influenced by his previous encounters.

Students with little or no previous movement experiences present the greatest challenge to the teacher's creativeness, and subsequently provide the true test of your expertise and ability to communicate. Unfortunately, disabled students are the ones most often forgotten. For one reason or another their experiences may have been limited. They may have become isolated and withdrawn from participating, causing them to reduce their efforts for fear of failure. Many of these students may have tried, but were influenced negatively by their experiences and the lack of care or experience on the part of their instructors. They may come wanting to learn, but harboring negative feelings. Bringing these to the surface requires establishing trust between both student and teacher. For the progress of the student it becomes almost imperative.

Previous Golf Experience

Previous experience in golf may become an important consideration when working with newly handicapped or disabled individuals. These considerations involve three primary aspects:
- the previous level of skill
- the modifications necessary because of the limitation
- the positive or negative effect of the experience.

Previous Level of Skill—An individual who was a 12 handicap golfer before being blinded in an industrial accident has a well established golf swing, and merely needs help lining up shots and orienting toward the pin. The shot characteristics will be similar to any other sighted player, and the adaptations will be related to the judgments of distance and alignment to the target.

In contrast, a former right handed golfer who suffered an accidental left arm amputation may have swing modifications necessary which might suggest a switch to a "left handed" orientation toward the pin, with the right arm on the target side. This change in orientation may initially seem quite difficult. But when you consider that the former 12 handicap golfer has already learned an effective swing, and how to generate force, and a general rhythm, it will be possible to capitalize on this past experience. With an understanding of the "mirror image" of the new swing from the old, the golfer may quickly adapt to this new direction.

Golfers who have previously established a solid golf swing will have this motor pattern stored in their memory. This motor plan, or schema, for a golf swing will provide a modifiable base for future golfing performance. That is, if a general concept of the golf swing has become a permanent part of this golfer's past experience, it should be used to help adjust to any new changes. These past skills should help this individual make the adjustments, if their initial skills were well learned. On the other hand, an individual with only limited past experience may have learned only "enough to be dangerous." Their limited past experience may have begun to lay only a skeleton golf swing. And to switch a "bare bones" skeleton is perhaps more difficult than making modifications in a well established motor skill.

Nature of Required Modifications—Individuals who are asked to make rather subtle modifications in their golf swings may have more problems understanding these changes than those who must change their swings dramatically. That is, some subtle changes cause confusion, and are hard to really "feel." On the other hand a golfer who must switch completely from one side to another, or from one grip to another, can easily focus on these changes.

When a golfer must make subtle changes in the swing, stance or grip, or ball placement, these changes may be difficult because of the previously learned style. This problem, referred to as negative transfer, requires careful consideration. Golfers will be able to make these changes easier if they understand the nature of the required modifications. If such a golfer knows that he should hold the club in such-and-such a way, there may be confusion as to the difference between the old and new requirements. Allow the golfer to experiment in the extremes to find the desired position. An example is that of helping the golfer establish a neutral grip position. Have the golfer hit shots with the target hand on top with 3 or 4 knuckles visible; reverse the position so that only 1 knuckle is visible. Now it should be easier to find the middle or neutral position of 2 to 2½ knuckles. Other examples are:

- A scratch golfer who becomes totally blind has the greatest adaptation in distance perception by kinesthetic feel.
- A 4-handicap golfer who loses his lower left leg will have few adaptations in his swing.

Previous Golf Experience: Positive or Negative

The more positive the past experience with golf the better. The student with positive past experiences is eager and more motivated. The reverse is true for the negative experience. If the previous exposures were negative, time must be spent selling golf and/or yourself, rather than merely providing a learning experience. But once the negative experience is overcome, the road becomes much smoother.

Whether the past experience in golf or the impact of the instructor was a positive or negative influence on the student is often difficult to determine. If the student feels positive about golf, it perhaps makes little difference. But, if negative, the past experience may need to be discussed in order to separate the instructor from experiences. The instructor plays a vital role in encouraging students and turning them on to or off an activity. Golf by itself may be a bore, with failure a likely outcome. Making the game challenging and exciting, viewing those failures in more positive ways, and motivating golfers to want to learn, is not always an easy task. But it can be done. It takes enthusiasm and a desire to share those positive experiences to make a difference to all students. They most certainly are a major consideration in the receptiveness of special populations even to attempt an activity such as golf. For example:

- Amputees have quit golf because instructors said they couldn't help them.
- A blind golfer who shot in the 80's has experienced the strong influence of an interested instructor.
- A paraplegic who plays from a golf cart and shoots in the 70's has related his love of the game and thrill of being out and free on the course.
- A congenital quadruple amputee, who is 22 years old and shoots in the high 80-'s, is a model of determination and desire to play the game.

Personal Desires for Playing Golf

The excitement and enthusiasm with which any individual enters an activity will often determine his ultimate success or failure. Golf is no exception, for in many respects, it may require more enthusiasm and dedication than other sports. Success in golf may not be as immediate and lasting as in other activities. It requires dedication and effort that many are not willing or not able to give. But success is not tangible and need not be defined in the same way for everyone. Shooting 70 one day and 68 the next may be success for one golfer, while for another, shooting 200 one day and 190 the next is equally exciting and successful.

As instructors, we must not impose our personal desires for success or our measures of personal success upon our students. We need to provide a means for helping individuals assess their own motives and skills for playing golf. We must help them identify what they initially view as success in relation to their own abilities. It might be important to go back to what has been alluded to as a measure of success—performance. Performance may only be a by-product of wanting to play golf for many individuals. But we often assume it is the only thing. Allow students to express their motives or desires verbally or otherwise. Not all students may have asked themselves "why" they want to learn golf. This time of introspection may provide you, as well as your student with additional insights.

Motives To Learn And/Or Play Golf

Is the attempt to learn golf the student's choice, or that of an outside agent (family, friends, doctor/therapist)? Those golfers who have made their own choice tend to "try" harder, exert more time and effort, maintain their enthusiasm and overcome their frustrations. Others just spend the time with little concerted effort and motivation, dwelling on frustrations with no impact from the successes.

The instructor's role is to help the student become aware of the many benefits of participation in golf. It is not merely the score of a round of golf that can provide a measure of success. The socialization, mental, emotional and physical fitness aspects should be fostered as well as continuous reinforcement for their effort. Encouraging a friend or family member to participate with the golfer might also be suggested in order to develop outside support and reinforcement. For example:

- A mentally retarded golfer and friend learn golf together.
- A one-handicap above the knee (A/K) amputee brings a discrimination suit against the ASGA for not being allowed to ride the last 18 holes of qualifying for the U.S. Open.
- The parents of a deaf mute join so they can take lessons together.

Expectations

The way a golfer feels about his own performance (i.e., his expectations), has two different implications. The first relates to future anticipation of success in golf, which may be formulated on hopes, dreams, and desires. The second implication is more evaluative, in which anticipation of or for the future is based upon present status and/or ability to meet the known demands or requirements of a given task or skill. More simply, if we ask students about their expectations for their golf experience and they have no means of evaluating their present or past skill ability, some unrealistic expectation may follow. The greater the backlog of experiences, golf or otherwise, the greater potential for a more realistic evaluation of expectations.

Special populations tend to have low expectations for themselves. Many have had past experiences which provide only memories of failure and resultant rejection by peers, possibly the family, and ultimately the self. They have little from their own perspective to raise their expectations. The causes for these failures may be innumerable. They may have been put in situations they were unable to handle physically, mentally, socially or emotionally. They may have been "closeted" by their family. They may have been ridiculed by their peers. They may have withdrawn from participation or lack experiences to draw upon in a variety of situations. Causation is difficult, if not impossible to pinpoint.

Expectations can be raised, however, through careful instruction which includes helping the golfer through a progression that fosters the development of success and attitudes toward achievement in golf. Goal setting is an important aspect in creating achievement motivation in students. For example:

- A current 5-handicap right side below the elbow (B/E) amputee wants to place in the top five in the National Amputee Tournament.
- A visually impaired 7-handicap golfer wants to get her handicap down to 4.
- A young deaf golfer wants to play well enough to join a parent on the course.
- A mentally retarded golfer just wants to get the ball airborne.

Goals

What do potential golfers want to accomplish? Limited or negative experience may result in either goals that are too high or too low. Realistic evaluation is difficult for all golfers and may be particularly hard for those who are disabled. However, it remains an important question. Many disabled are able to evaluate accurately what they're capable of doing as well as those things which may seem a little out of reach. Others may tend to shy away from the challenges. Each individual should be considered separately in terms of goals, with guidance provided in establishing goals. The amount of guidance will vary with each person. Consideration should be given to goal-setting and perhaps clarification of their purpose. Basically, goal-setting is one means of increasing motivation. The motivation to achieve may be for intrinsic and/or extrinsic gratification. The goals should be specific in nature and stated in measurable terms of time and quantity.

Goal-setting should be viewed with respect to building a ladder—not just any ladder, but one with a set number of rungs and height. Each ladder is specific to an individual. The desired height will be the long-term goal for which the individual is striving. The rungs represent short-term goals which are the steps to be set and reached en route to the top or desired end. The distance between the rungs and the number of rungs may vary for each individual. Each rung, or short-term goal, helps to build and establish success patterns. These patterns provide continuing positive reinforcement and encouragement for the effort expended.

Each time a short-term goal is reached, a new goal is set that leads to the eventual long-term goal. This provides an on-going process of evaluation and re-evaluation of ability. Within the process of goal-setting (Table 6.2), exciting things are happening for the individual and instructor. The individual is growing with respect to learning and understanding more about himself, his capabilities and limitations. Establishing and reaching short-term goals through a system of progressions which are challenging, yet not out of reach, creates success opportunities which many individuals may not have experienced in other endeavors. With the development of a more positive self-awareness, the desire to achieve should enhance the individual's desire to assume more responsibility for their actions and to gain a higher degree of independence.

Table 6.2
Suggested Techniques for Goal Setting

State the desired long-term goal:
- To break 100 in three months (presently averaging 120).

Identify strengths and weaknesses:
- Strengths—hitting fairly straight and good wood player.
- Weakness—Short approaches (25 yards and in), putting (average 45 putts).

Be realistic, sequential and progressive

Short Term Goals:
- To reduce the number of strokes around the green (present average 3/hole) to 2 within three months.
- To reduce putting average from 45 putts/round to 36 within three months.

Suggested Sequence for Reducing the Number of Approach Shots Using 7-9 Irons:
- Week 1: Develop good stroke techniques for first week, work only on technique (mechanics of stroke: Ex. Triangle-track-target concept).
  (After first week devote first ¼ of practice to techniques)
- Week 2: Develop feel for distance from 10 yards out. The goal is to hit 7 of 10 shots to within 7 feet of the pin.
- Week 3: Continue working on feel for distance from 15 yards out. The goal is to hit 5 of 10 shots to within 7 feet of the pin.

Last ¼ of practice alternate shots between 10 and 15 yards out. Goal is to get within 7 points of the pin.

   In the minds of most instructors, individuals come to us to learn golf. They're motivated and dedicated to excel. Not always true! We must take time to get to know our students. We must take the initiative to listen, observe and establish an open communication system with each individual. We can't assume anything about someone else's needs and desires. We must ask. Assessment allows us a means to begin communication—to express an interest in each individual and to gain insight into what is the best and the most efficient method for maximizing that individual's potential.

CHAPTER 7

Communicating With The Golfer

by Greg Shasby

Teaching golf to individuals with various types of handicapping conditions is a challenging and rewarding task. In analyzing the process of teaching, emphasis should be placed on the communication that takes place between golfer and teacher. The type of communication will be determined by principles of learning and performance applicable to all individuals. Particular handicaps, however, require that the communication process be refined to enhance learning.

Clarifying the meaning of communication is important in understanding the teacher-learner relationship. Communication involves the sharing of information, thoughts and feelings so they are satisfactorily received and understood. As a process, communication involves an exchange of information between individuals through a common system of language: both verbal and nonverbal. The emphasis is on the receiving end of communication. The key involves finding the correct system of communication to allow the student and teacher to exchange information about a common goal effectively. In this case, it is the learning and performance of a new motor skill—golf.

The two principle objectives of communication in teaching golf are: establishing the goals of performance (identifying the specific skill or skills to be learned), and giving feedback about performance to correct errors and reinforce appropriate performance.

To deal systemically with the objectives of establishing goals and providing for performance evaluation, a model (Figure 7.1) for learning skills, adapted from Martenuik,[1] will be used to emphasize specific components of the teacher-learner process. The components will be discussed in general and then specifically as they relate to particular handicapping conditions in later sections.

---

1. Martenuik, R.G. *Information Processing in Motor Skills.* New York: Holt, Rinehart and Winton, 1976.

Figure 7.1 Communication Model for Teaching Golf*

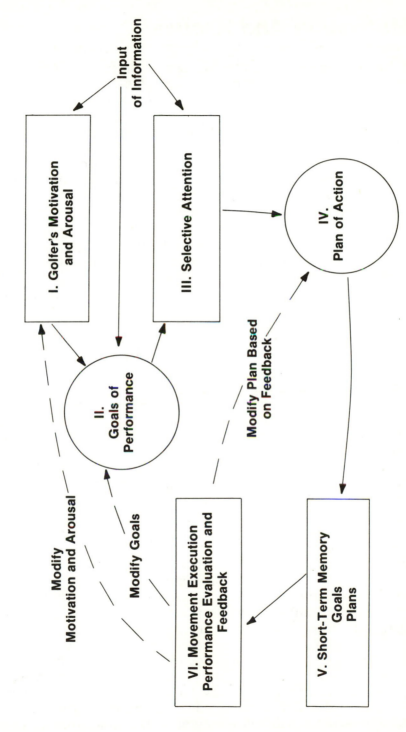

*Adapted from Martenuik, 1976.

Motivation And Arousal

Each individual golfer comes with his own level of motivation. Motivation and arousal deal with the state of the individual in terms of readiness and willingness to engage actively in the learning process. If the learner is not alert and motivated to learn, the teaching process will not be successful, no matter how well it is structured.

Each golfer's arousal level can be thought of as the amount of excitement in the nervous system. An individual's arousal level can vary from a very low point (deep sleep) to a very high level (associated with extreme excitement or anxiety). Arousal level is critically associated with our ability to recognize (perceive) and use information received from our body and outside our body in directing motor performance.

An analogy will be used to make the relationship between arousal and the ability to perceive information and therefore communicate understandably more clear. Imagine yourself in a totally dark room sitting in a chair, facing a wall with a picture of a forest scene on it. The task you are presented is to identify the specific type of flower growing in the meadow. The totally dark situation (deep sleep) permits no information to be obtained from the picture. Gradually, the intensity of the light in the room is increased to a point where you can begin to recognize shapes on the wall, but not distinguish distinct features. Therefore, no usable information relative to the task is being received. As the light continues to increase in intensity, visual patterns emerge and the picture begins to take shape although it is still a vague representation of the actual picture and much information in the form of detail needed to identify the flowers is lost. The light continues to increase in intensity to the point where optimal viewing of the picture occurs. The goal of recognizing particular shapes and colors is now possible and the ability to do so optimal. Detail becomes vivid and all the information in the picture is available to us for an accurate image of the scene. This is the ideal learning and performance situation relative to the flower identification task. If the light were to continue to increase in intensity we would again begin to lose our ability to see all the details of the picture as glare would become a factor. The picture would become washed as does a photo taken in bright sunlight without the proper aperture adjustment. This situation represents overarousal and results again in a loss of information.

In actuality, the control for the light intensity, is in our own brain. The level of light, representing nervous system stimulation, should not be too low or too high, but at a level permitting us to perceive and process the information needed in the learning and performance of a particular motor skill. Each individual has his or her own optimal or "best" level of arousal relative to personality characteristics and level of learning in relation to the new learning task.

Motivation directly affects arousal and therefore our potential for optimal learning and performance. Motivation is affected by the relevance of the goal or activity. Relevance is associated with the golfer's ability to perceive the goal or activity as important, interesting and worth the effort. It will also effect the level of persistence exhibited in learning the activity and the intensity or amount of effort put forth. The more desirable the goal, the higher the level of motivation and arousal.

The process of goal identification plays an essential role in setting the stage for effective communication to take place between the student and teacher. Once the general goal (i.e., to learn to play golf) has been identified as meaningful and important to the learner, the teacher can then assume the student will come with at least an adequate level of arousal.

The next step is to break down the general goal into more specific goals (i.e., full swing, short shots, and putting), which will be used in the motor skill learning process. These goals will not only determine content but provide short term goals for motivation during each lesson. They become critically important when the larger goal may be too big, or too long term for some individuals to understand.

The essential elements of communication involve the identification of both long term and short term goals by the student and teacher. Both teacher and learner should agree on their purpose and the importance of each goal before beginning a series of lessons.

Formulation Of The Goals Of Performance

In the goal formulation stage we begin to take a closer look at the short term goals identified in the previous stage. These short term goals become the very specific content of the learning experience. The teacher must communicate the specific skill either through verbal explanation, video or demonstration methods or any combination of these. This process of goal clarification serves several functions: It directs the learner's attention and it can be used as an important motivational tool to enhance learning and performance.

The communication that takes place also affects how the golfer will formulate a plan of action to be used in a later stage. A plan of action is the idea or image of the movement in the student's head (for example, executing a full swing with a 5-iron). The image gives the golfer a basis for developing an actual movement sequence to accomplish the task.

Goal identification and clarification also helps to focus our attention. The goal helps select the various aspects of performance specifically related to the task at hand. Focusing attention in this way simplifies learning by reducing the quantity of information that has to be handled. Less information makes communication easier and more precise.

Good communication in setting goals helps establish proper motivation and arousal, the formulation of a plan of action, and the focusing of attention on specific details of the performance.

Selective Attention

Selective attention involves the process of focusing one's attention on certain aspects of the learning process. Specific direction of attention is central to the performance of the identified skill. If you are working on grip or stance or a particular type of shot, the objective is for the golfer to pay particular attention to that element of the skill while it is being learned. For example, if the skill is chipping, specific attention could be given to the backward and forward swing as having equal length. (*Key:* distance back = distance through). One of the best ways to direct this attention is to remind the golfer of the goals previously set.

There are several characteristics of attention which need to be understood to control it effectively during learning. First, we have a limited ability to pay attention to information. The saying "You can't pay attention to two things at once" is true but needs to be qualified. What this means is that you can't give your full attention to one event and expect to gain information from another. This is a common source of conflict for the student and teacher when the student's orientation is with the results (product) and the teacher is trying to direct the student to the feel (process) of the stroke. The most basic element in communication is therefore getting the golfer's attention. When a student is not paying attention, he or she is not receiving the proper instructions, and accordingly cannot establish goals and focus attention. In addition, feedback from his or her performance is not obtained.

In the early stages of learning a motor skill, the number of instructions to which a student must pay attention should be limited. Emphasize only those which are associated with the specific skill at hand. This can be done by employing some of the other principles of attention.

Attention can be directed in two ways basically. First, attention can be consciously and actively focused on something specific. Individuals pay attention to something by choice. To focus attention effectively in this way, the object of attention must have been identified beforehand. As in the previous example, if the process or the feeling of the stroke is the attentional focus, the student should be made aware that this would require him to focus in on how his body was feeling during the swing motion (i.e. restricted, free, effortless, etc.). The student must be familiar enough with the object to differentiate and select it from all the possible information presented. The process presupposes that some learning has taken place allowing the student to select the appropriate information.

The less an individual is able to direct attention consciously, the more important the second attentional focusing process becomes. This process is a more automatic, natural focus which occurs when attention is drawn to something because of the nature of its qualities. Brightness, loudness, colorfulness, unusualness, and meaningfulness are some examples of qualities which automatically attract attention.

In the early stages of learning, depending on the individual's ability to focus attention consciously, the more automatic techniques of attention control should be utilized. As the student begins to build a memory for golf, he will find it easier to focus attention through the use of verbal or sign cues. The cue response can be estalished early by always associating a particular cue ("back-through") with the specific attentional focus (length of stroke). As any one aspect of the golf swing is learned through practice, it will require less attentional effort and new aspects of the skill can become the center of attention.

Formulating The Plan Of Action

The fourth step, formulating the plan of action, involves communicating to the students the component parts of the skill and how they are organized and "sequenced" in performance. Both the overall idea (product and process) and the component parts of the movement must be clear in order to execute the movement and then compare the outcome with the idea or plan.

Each previous step lays the foundation for developing a clear image or plan. Students should be actively involved in preparing for the performance of the skill. Preparation can be enhanced by telling students to describe verbally what must be done and/or imagine the performance of the skill.

The objective of communication at this stage is to insure that the golfer is actively prepared to execute a golf swing. It is essential that the teacher receive communication from the student relative to the active process of formulating the plan to insure that the plan is a correct one.

Short Term Memory

Effective communication requires not only that the information be received by the learner but also that it be retained for use in the learning and performance of the skill. Understanding some general principles about golf will help each individual learn to be a self-corrector. The Laws, Principles and Preferences described in Chapter 2 provide an excellent tool for improving short term memory.

Information that is familiar to the student is more easily retained than totally new information. Pointing out similarities between the new skill and past experiences can aid in this process. For example, the pitch shot motion may be perceived as one-half of the full swing motion.

It is also important to keep the student's attention focused on the important material. This can be accomplished in several ways. The time period between the presentation of goals, development of selective attention, generation of a plan of action, and the actual performance should be kept short. The student will then not have as much time to forget.

Another technique to improve learning is rehearsal. Students should either verbally or mentally repeat the instructions or plans for carrying out the activity. This type of rehearsal will help retain the important information in short term memory so it can be used in directing the movement. For example, after instructions are given, have the golfer imagine the perfect swing, or verbally describe what they will attempt to do.

The objective of this short term memory component is to insure that the communication carried on in the previous stages is retained and fully used in the execution of the motor skill.

Movement Execution And Feedback

When the learner actually performs the skill (executes the plan of action), a number of events occur. The learner is initially concerned with producing the planned movement. To facilitate this, be sure there are no distracting things in the environment. Distractions can be anything which would divert the golfer's focus of attention. Examples might be noise, attractive objects, nearby movement, the sun in the golfer's eyes, or anything unusual that would attract attention and disrupt concentration. Other distractors might include unresolved personal problems brought to the lesson which take attention away from the peformance goals.

Once the skill is executed two questions related to performance need to be answered. One concerns whether the movement was executed according to the plan of action. The second concerns whether the goal of the movement was achieved. The student needs to receive information about both questions. Positive reinforcement should be given for a correct performance, or specific changes in the plan of action should be recommended before the next attempt.

Precise information about performance is essential if learning is to take place. The performance itself can be evaluated by the student or teacher, or both. The student can be directed to pay attention to certain aspects of the swing or the results of the performance. This information must be appropriate for the special needs of each golfer.

Table 7.1
Summary of Instructional Considerations* for Special Populations

	Physically Impaired	Visually Impaired	Hearing Impaired	Mentally Impaired
Movement Limitation	Yes/No	No	No	No
Movement Deviations from Normal	Yes/No	No	No	No
Normal Movement Experiences	Yes/No	Yes	Yes/No	Yes/No
Average Intelligence	Yes	Yes	Yes	Yes/No
Information Processing				
Motivation	No	Yes	No	Yes
Goals of Performance	No	Yes	No	Yes
Selective Attention	No	Yes	No	Yes
Plan of Action	No	Yes	No	Yes
Short Term Memory	No	Yes	No	Yes
Movement Execution & Feedback	No	Yes	No	Yes
Performance Evaluative	No	Yes	No	Yes

*Considerations relate to similarities and differences between special populations and non-impaired peers.

No = no differences
Yes = differences

Table 7.1 (continued)
Summary of Instructional Considerations for Special Populations

	Physically Impaired	Visually Impaired	Hearing Impaired	Mentally Impaired
Institution Emphasis				
Verbal	Yes	Yes	No	Yes
Modeling (mimic)	Yes	No	Yes	Yes
Demonstrative	Yes	No	Yes	Yes
Manipulative	Yes	Yes	Yes	Yes
Tactile	Yes	Yes	Yes	Yes
Kinesthetic	Yes	Yes	Yes	Yes
Sign	No	No	Yes	No
Instruction Time	No	No	No	No/Yes
Golf swing Deviation	Yes/No	No	No	No
Specific Considerations				
Golf Instruction	Yes/No	Yes	Yes	Yes
Golf Swing Deviation	Yes/No	No	No	No
Safety (suggest play with non-impaired partner)	Yes/No	Yes	Yes	Yes

Summary

Ideas for teaching selected groups of individuals (mentally retarded, physically impaired, blind-visually impaired, and deaf-hearing impaired) with handicapping conditions can be easily applied using the model (Figure 7.1) discussed in this chapter. The following chapters will use this model in relation to a specific handicapping condition. Each chapter will also include suggestions for implementing the model in golf instruction. It is important to note that there are two general areas of instructional concern: the mechanics of the swing, and the communication skills used to share information with each golfer. The actual mechanical techniques (Chapters 4 and 5) may or may not be the same with all golfers.

Similarly, the communication of the techniques and/or the communication with the golf student may require some modification or change. A guide for potential instructional considerations is presented in Summary in Table 7.1. Each golfer must be considered individually by evaluating their
- motivation
- goals of performance
- attention
- ability to plan and execute a skill
- availability of information or feedback about this execution.

CHAPTER 8

Mental Retardation

by Greg Shasby

Mental retardation is a general term describing a range of intellectual and adaptive behavior which is below what is considered to be normal. Significantly subaverage general intellectual functioning refers to performance which is more than two standard deviations from the mean as measured by a formal intelligence test (the normal IQ = 84 and above, while mentally retarded scores are less than 84). Adaptive behavior is defined as the effectiveness or degree to which the individual meets the standards of personal independence and social responsibility expected of his age and cultural group.

The range of retardation is divided into four subcategories that describe the extent of the disability. The four categories are mild, moderate, severe, and profound retardation. The mild and moderate will be the focus of attention, for these two groups are the ones most likely to be encountered in golf instruction.

Model

Motivation—Each individual's level of motivation is extremely important when teaching the retarded. As a general rule, the more severe the level of retardation, the more the teacher will have to become directly and actively involved in motivating the student. Since a major part of motivation comes from thoughts and cognitive functions, a mentally retarded golfer may be unable to conceptualize the purpose and importance of the long range goal of playing golf on the golf course. Short term goals such as developing a putting stroke and sinking 5 out of 10 putts from 5 feet with immediate rewards take on increased significance. The greater the degree of retardation, the more concrete and immediate the goals and rewards must become.

Concreteness comes from visual input such as pictures, graphs and charts which allow the student to visualize the goal. Praise and rewards for their behavior might be best in the form of stars, checks or tokens. The key is to develop and maintain motivation through

- goal identification
- goal clarification
- goal attainment
- goal recognition.

Students need to see themselves succeed and improve over time and need to have this occur in a clearly defined way.

The source of motivation may be external to the student, thus necessitating a very active and effective communication exchange between the teacher and pupil. Goals of performance must be very specific—for example, to chip 5 balls within 10 feet—and communicated in a clear, but simple way. The teacher must pay particular attention to the golfer's response to directions and instructions. The response of the student is the true test of the effectiveness of the communication and therefore the teacher's most important source of feedback. Continued motivation will come only through proper feedback, which enables the student to see change and improvement in performance relative to the identified goals.

Goals of Performance—The importance of establishing performance goals in order to help the students learn specific golf skills was previously mentioned. This stage is concerned with the process of using the goals to directly guide the student's skill development. The focus here is specifically on methods of effectively communicating and setting goals that will result in the desired movement.

It is necessary to be selective in the manner of communicating information relative to the identified goals. The retarded student is limited in the ability to deal with a variety of sensory communication input. Two methods seem to be of greatest value. First, the retarded golfer is generally a very good imitator. Images provide very strong directions for behavior. When working with young retarded golfers, this would suggest that verbalizing should be minimized, with more emphasis placed on simple demonstration, the use of pictures and videotapes, for example. Seeing a demonstration may communicate more usable information for directing movement than verbally describing the activity. The retarded student can use the visual information to function as a directive in movement.

The visual input (in the form of a demonstration) should be accompanied or paired with some type of cue so the student can recall the image when given the cue rather than having to repeat the demonstration. For example, the instructor can swing with the golfer (mirror) with verbal cues "back and through." Visual input can be gradually faded to verbal cues which in turn will be faded.

A second useful method involves actually physically guiding the student through the desired movement (manipulation). Through this process the student can begin to feel what the movement is like and therefore gain a better understanding of the movement goal. When the demonstration or manipulation takes place, the student's attention should also be directed to an appropriate picture or chart which illustrates the particular point or goal. The student will later return to this graphic display and chart his own progress, reinforcing the specific new learning.

Selective Attention—Selective attention is the ability to focus attention on particular points of the swing and/or strategy that is important to successfully swing the club and/or play the course. The retarded have a particular inability to direct attention to specific aspects of the learning task. Since the secondary or voluntary attentional abilities depend on conceptualization, the retarded will be limited in being able to consciously direct attention. Primary or automatic attentional mechanisms will play a larger role in determining attentional focus and therefore determining performance and feedback.

The first consideration is with the immediate environment (i.e. brightness, loudness, colorfulness, unusualness, meaningfulness). If primary attentional mechanisms are going to dominate, then it is important to reduce any sensory input from the environment that would distract the golfer's attention.

The physical size of the environment can be important. If possible a smaller area is beneficial in the early stages of learning (i.e. indoor area or a quiet area or portion of a driving range or field). The smaller area allows for better control over the potentially distracting influences, making it easier for the golfer to direct attention to the task at hand.

Limiting extraneous sensory information helps golfers gain control over the primary attention mechanism. Instructors should use those qualities which naturally attract attention in the teaching process. Through the use of color, sound, novelty, visually attractive objects and tactile input, the teacher can focus the student's attention on a particular aspect of learning to swing. The teacher should also establish a cue (example, back and through) with the specific focus of attention. As the student begins to learn to focus attention through repetition, use of the cue will result in the focused attention being brought under conscious control. As secondary attentional mechanisms are developed, the need for primary attentional techniques are reduced. At the same time the enclosed, controlled environment becomes less important due to the increased ability to voluntarily focus attention with the additional aid of the cues. External stimuli should have a reduced effect in competing for attention as concentration or the ability to focus attention improves.

The key to effective communication in this stage involves establishing
- control of attention by reducing irrelevant stimuli
- increasing the strength of attention-attracting properties in key elements of the task
- through the use of cues facilitating the development of voluntary attention control.

Plan of Action—Some special considerations are important for preparing the student to actually execute the skill. Communication focuses on providing the golfer with an appropriate step by step understanding of the movement sequence and the movement goal for executing the golf swing.

Demonstration and manual manipulation may be the most effective way to communicate the movement to be accomplished. It is important, however, to determine how much of the skill should be taught at any one time. The golf swing (full, short, and putt) can be broken down into steps or component parts and therefore taught in segments and gradually integrated together to eventually constitute the total movement skill (see Chapter 4 and 5). Although breaking the swing down into component parts simplifies the task, each time the component parts are linked together it represents a new learning step. A retarded golfer may have trouble sequencing complex movement. Therefore, teaching the swing in as large a unit as possible but within the student's ability to perform a movement sequence will produce the best results.

All golfers need time to process a command or suggestion and generate a response. The processing time for the mentally retarded golfer requires much effort and results in fatigue. The amount of new learning should be spaced over time to allow for processing and recovery. As the student becomes more familiar with the swing, it requires less effort, so new information can be added and practice time extended.

To aid the student in carrying out the skill the setting should be simplified. This can be accomplished, for example, by
- instructing the student on how to arrange himself relative to the task
- the order of the task
- specifics on the manipulation of objects.

Clearly defining boundaries, color coding goals, and setting up patterns of movement with tape on the floor are additional ways to simplify the task by directing the student's action with external cues and signals.

Short-Term Memory—In order to be sure the student will retain the information to successfully execute the swing, several techniques can be used. Establishing the cues to direct attention and signal appropriate movement sequences in the earlier phases will make it easier to elicit the proper response in this phase. The teacher should actively cue the student to stimulate the attentional focus and memory of movement prior to execution. Cue rehearsal (verbalization) by the student can also be encouraged with the teacher prompting the student on the appropriate cue sequence. Examples of cues are right-left, back-through, or motion back-motion through.

Movement Execution and Feedback—When the student actually executes the movement skill, cueing and feedback during the movement and feedback after the movement performance can aid the student in maintaining the proper movement sequence. Feedback after the performance reinforces the desired performance and permits the student to perceive change and success relative to the goal. This aids in the motivational component and encourages future practice for additional learning.

The goal of the teaching process is to get the golfer to the point where the skills are retained over a period of time. Retention is best when an optimum degree of overlearning has been used. Overlearning involves having the student repeat the skill a number of times after being successful. The determination of success (the criterion) comes from the specific goals established in earlier phases of the teaching process (i.e. making 5 out of 10 putts from 5 feet).

CHAPTER 9

Golf Instruction For The Mentally Retarded

by DeDe Owens

The following unit outline for beginning golfers who are mentally retarded is designed for rapid initial learning with minimal equipment. It can be taught in a gymnasium or field area. It is recommended that groups be limited in size (4-6 students or less depending upon instructor expertise). This is particularly important for mixed groups because of the need for individual attention and supervision. Additional help can be quite beneficial and might include interested paraprofessionals or non-impaired students as partners. This could be an excellent joint experience in a mainstreamed physical education setting or community environment.

The design of this unit assumes that the students are mentally retarded, but have normal physical capacities (no physical disabilities). Their potential for motion is the same as for other non-impaired golfers. The instructional techniques presented in Chapters 4 and 5 are appropriate for this group. One of the major concerns is in the area of communications, as discussed in the preceding section. Particular emphasis should focus on

- simplicity in cues
- repetition
- modeling
- goal setting
- reinforcement
- part-whole learning sequences.

The suggested golf sequence begins with putting and progresses through the full swing. The purpose is to

- develop immediate success patterns in contacting the ball (=motivation)
- to develop an arm swing and body flow awareness in order to foster more club control.

The range of individual learning rates and potential of golfers with mild and moderate mental retardation is quite wide. This unit was designed for a typical MR student, though many students may progress at a faster or slower pace than the unit suggests. Accordingly, this unit should be used only as a guide, to be modified at the discretion of the instructor. It should be tailored to fit the specific needs of the individual student.

The typical golf lesson program presented in the Appendix differs from the suggested MR unit in the sequencing of skills and the number of lessons. As has been emphasized, these units are guides. It would be beneficial for the instructor to use the lesson breakdown of the typical golf lesson as a reference and supplement lecture aspects as desired with the MR golfers.

Suggested Golf Unit
Beginning MR

	Equipment	Objectives
LESSON 1 **Putting**	Putters (different lengths) Putting cups (or targets) Golf Balls Putting carpet/smooth rug 2 x 4's Putting aids	To have fun Technique development (grip/stance/posture) Develop feel of club-ball contact Develop feel of swing length (back/forward)
LESSON 2 **Review**	Same as above	To reinforce objective #1 To develop sense of target and distance GOALS: Hit target: 4 of 10 from 5 feet Hit target: 4 of 10 from 8 feet
LESSON 3 **Review** **Putting**	Same as above Course, if possible Putting stations with varying distances Specific goals at each with reward	To reinforce #1 and #2 To develop awareness of distance changes with swing length

	Equipment	Objectives

LESSON 4
Short shot
(5 to 7 swing)
	Plastic balls (inside)
	Carpet stripes
	Aids*
	Putter/9 iron**
		To understand differences in putter and lofted club:
		  Design
		  Use
		  Trajectory
		GOALS:
		  To hit the wall above a line 2 feet from the floor (4 of 10 times)
		  To hit over an object 4 feet in front of wall (4 of 10 times)
		To develop a feel of the stroke (back/forward)

LESSON 5 **Short Shot** **(7 to 5)**	Same Wall targets***	Same as #4 To develop target awarness GOAL: to hit target 4 of 10 times
Introduce		To develop feel for longer stroke To understand swing length and resulting distance To develop target awareness with 8 to 4 lengths if progress warrants
LESSON 6 **Short Shot** **(8 to 4)**	Same as 5	Same as lesson 5 Target emphasis GOAL: to hit target 8 feet away 4 of 10 times
Review **Putting**	Putting station	Same as lesson 3
LESSON 7 **Review** **Short Shots** **(5 to 7)**	Same	To distinguish swing lengths for different distances

*Age appropriate targets (younger students could use colors/letters/numbers, to reinforce classroom learning), and aids (Appendix).
**Clubs of varying length and weight to fit individual's height and strength.
***Appendix.

	Equipment	Objectives
LESSON 7 (cont'd) Introduce 7 iron (5 to 7) (8 to 4)	Variety of stations and targets	To understand choice of club loft to go x-distance and x-height
LESSON 8 Review Short Shots Putt (5 to 7) (* to 4)	Using different colors, hoops, ropes, the wall stations calling for clubs and trajectory distance Set up stations with no choice of clubs Set up stations with desire of clubs	Target awareness
LESSON 9 Introduce ½ Swing (Directed Motion without necessary target)	9 iron, plastic balls mats, lines on floor or mats	Develop arm's swinging motion lower body Motion without concern target but with alignment
LESSON 10 Swing ½ Swing	Same	Same as #9 Add targets Motion 1st
LESSON 11 Review ½ Swing	Same	Motion Accuracy
LESSON 12 Review Short Swing	Same	Same Change lengths of swing/ purpose Targets different distances
LESSON 13 Introduce Full Swing	5-iron, mats, plastic or golf ball	Motion First
LESSON 14 Review Full Swing	Same	Motion

	Equipment	Objectives
LESSON 15 **Review** **Full Swing**	Same	Motion Target awareness GOAL: to hit 4 of 10 balls wihin a target area 30 yards wide
LESSON 16 **Review** **Full Swing** **Introduce** **Full Swing** **with Woods**	Fairway woods with loft (4,5, or 6), tees, plastic or golf balls	Motion
LESSON 17 **Review** **Full Swing** **Short Swing**	Woods (above) and irons (5,7, 9)	Motion Target awareness GOAL: To hit 4 of 10 balls within an area 40 yards wide
LESSON 18 **Take a Course** **Play a Hole**	3 clubs per student (wood, iron putter)	FUN Realization of long-term goal (to play golf on a course)

CHAPTER 10

Visually And Hearing Impaired

by Greg Shasby

Visually Impaired

Visual handicaps are defined in terms of visual acuity as measured by a Snellen chart. Legal blindness begins at 20/200 where the individual has the ability to see at 20 feet what the normal eye can see at 200 feet. The progressive loss of vision extends to being limited only to the perception of motion, to perceiving only bright light, to total blindness. Current classification of visual handicap stresses functional ability. Individuals who cannot read print and must be taught braille are classified as blind while others with less involvement and able to read print are considered visually impaired.

Blindness and visual impairment are largely problems of old age. Of the half million persons in the United States who are legally blind, at least two-thirds are over sixty-five years of age. Approximately one out of every 1000 children between the ages of five and nineteen are visually impaired or blind.

Model

An overall understanding of the game of golf is important in motivating the golfer and helping him associate specific types of learning with the purpose and objectives of the game. For the blind and more severely visually impaired who are unable to see a golf course and someone playing golf, a physical model can be used. The physical model should have a variety of tactile surfaces to aid in developing an overall concept of the layout of a golf course and terminology associated with the various parts such as the fairway, rough, bunker, green, etc. Associating the terminology with the different components and then relating the parts to each other is very important in developing a working understanding of the course. Moving an object representing a ball around the model course can aid in developing the concept of the number of strokes used in a game and begins to introduce the idea of different types of shots. The idea of different ball

Figure 10.1   Charlie Boswell, former National Blind Champion and his assistant. (courtesy *Birmingham News*)

tactile-kinesthetic input being received from the movement. The golfer must also receive feedback about the appropriateness of the movement pattern so that the proper tactile-kinesthetic memory can be developed. In the early stages of learning without some type of augmented feedback from the teacher or a physical aid, the blind golfer has no way to compare his performance with the desired one. Once the correct tactile-kinesthetic memory is developed, the memory can be used to establish the desired performance model.

With the blind golfer, the goals of performance are established through the plan of action stage. Establishing a clear plan of action requires feedback about performance with selective attention to certain aspects of body mechanics recognized through tactile-kinesthetic impressions. Over repeated trials the desired tactile-kinesthetic memory is established and used in executing future strokes.

Once the basic stroke is learned, only a few pieces of information about the specific shot are needed to effectively execute the movement. Establishing proper foot position to the hole or direction of the shot will require some assistance. Judging distance from the hole to determine club selection and shot characteristics will also need to be provided by an outside source. After the shot has been taken the resulting action and placement of the ball should be reported to the blind golfer so that minor adjustments for future shots can be made if necessary.

Hearing Impaired

Golf represents an excellent sport for the hearing impaired as it requires no outside auditory input for its performance. During instruction however, some communication system may be required.

Hearing impairment, like other disabilities, has a continuum of involvement. The ability to hear and perceive speech sounds is measured by the ability to pick up a certain intensity of sound. The unit of measurement which expresses the intensity of a sound is the decibel. Individuals with mild (20-30 decibel loss), marginal (30-40 decibel loss), moderate (40-60 decibel loss) and severe (60-90 decibel loss) losses are considered hearing impaired. The mild and marginal individual can learn normally if special attention is given to clear, strong speech and the use of a hearing aid.

The moderately involved individual can perceive some speech sounds with the help of a hearing aid, or phrases and words through loud conversation within about a three foot range. Caution must be taken because the hearing impaired may misunderstand phrases or words. The addition of lip reading and sign language are important to give a more complete understanding to spoken communication. This is particularly important for the severely and profoundly impaired, who will depend almost entirely on lip reading and signs for their trajectories can be developed by having the blind golfer move the ball through different trajectories with one hand while maintaining contact with the takeoff and landing points with the other. Discussion of the use and importance of different shots resulting in different trajectories and the consequent action of the ball can take place when it becomes appropriate to the developmental level of the golfer.

Goals of Performance, Selective Attention, Plan of Action, Feedback—Establishing specific instructional goals related to stroke production requires some general concept of the movement pattern to be used. Under normal circumstances, two types of sensory input are principally responsible for directing movement in specific patterned ways. Visual input in the form of visual images presents the most detailed information about the specific movement task and the environment around the performer. The second source of sensory input is tactile-kinesthetic input providing information about the body and the position of the body and its parts at any point in time. Ordinarily vision works in close cooperation with tactile-kinesthetic input to develop a memory of movement patterns permitting the organization and reproduction of very exacting movement.

The loss of vision then, either partially or totally eliminates one of the two principle sources of information used in the learning and performance of movement skills. The individual with partial sight has the ability, through the use of various visual aids (see Appendix) to develop a visual image of the movements required in golf and the spatial arrangements of the golf course. The clarity of the image and therefore the usefulness of the visual information will depend on the degree of visual impairment ranging from good to very poor.

Totally blind individuals can be divided into two groups with respect to the ability to use visual imagery in guiding movement and understanding spatial relationships. Those blind from birth do not have the ability to use visual imagery. Their understanding of the physical world comes through the tactile-kinesthetic impressions gained through active physical exploration. Describing the movements or physical relationships in terms of visual images has little meaning. The movements and relationships must be felt and physically experienced. Those individuals who were originally sighted and later became blind will have the ability to think in terms of images and can use the images to aid in directing movement and understanding spatial relationships.

For the totally blind, particularly in the initial stages of learning, special emphasis must be placed on developing a feeling for the form of the stroke. The memory of a particular pattern of tactile-kinesthetic input associated with a specific movement pattern must be developed. In order to develop a clear and accurate memory, two factors must be present. The student's attention must be focused on the communication.

Model

The learning model presented in the first part of this section can be applied to the hearing impaired and deaf without modification. The most important new skill that the instructor needs to acquire is the ability to communicate through the use of sign language such as key concepts and ideas related to the learning of golf. The communication techniques needed to teach golf to hearing impaired and deaf can be accomplished through gesture, direct reference to objects and body parts, some specific signs and finger spelling or writing. The American Manual Alphabet follows (Table 10.1). Additional key concepts and ideas are also presented in Table 10.2. The list is far from complete; however, it will be a beginning. Many of the ideas and concepts do not have signs and must be demonstrated or spelled using the manual alphabet.

Table 10.1 The American Manual Alphabet

SEE

The right "V" hand is held with the finger tips near the eyes, and the hand is brought forward and outward from the face. The reverse movement, that is, the finger tips jabbed toward the eyes, means BLIND. A wide variety of meanings can be expressed by this sign depending on how it is executed, e.g., STARE, LOOK SOMEONE OVER, LOOK AT ME, LOOK AROUND, LOOK UP, etc.

FINGERSPELLING, FINGERSPELL

The right "5" hand is held, palm down, in front of the body, and the fingers are wiggled. The hand may move from left to right as the sign is executed, but then the meaning may be restricted to SPELL OUT A WORD rather than FINGERS-PELLING in general. Originally this sign was reserved exclusively for FINGERSPELLING by means of the manual alphabet used by deaf people, but it is now used for SPELLING in the common sense of the word.

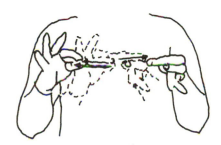

STORY, EXPLAIN, EXPLANATION

The thumbs and index finger of both "F" or "G" hands are interlocked and drawn apart several times. A prolonged or exaggerated gesture implies that a story or explanation went on on interminably. If the hands are drawn apart once in an alternating, twisting movement, the sign means SENTENCE, or, with "L" hands, LAN-GUAGE. If the "F" hands are moved alternately forward and backward in a horizontal plane in front of the body, with the tips of the thumb and middle fingers rubbing as they pass each other, the sign means DESCRIBE. The same sign executed with enlarged movements means EXPLAIN. EXPLAIN.

STOP

The left arm is held horizontally in front of the body, palm up, and the edge of the right hand, palm facing left, is struck into the left palm. The sign can also be used as an imperative. "Stop that."

Table 10.2 Manual Concepts

Reprinted with permission of Hoemann, H., Hofmann, S. *Sign Language Flash Cards.* Maryland: National Association of the Deaf. 1975.

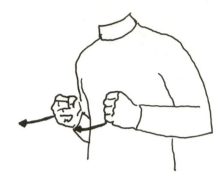

AGAIN

The left hand is held with the palm toward the face of the signer, and the fingertips of the right bent "B" hand are brought up and then into the palm of the left hand, the fingertips striking its center. If an abbreviated version of the sign is repeated frequently, it means OFTEN, i.e., again and again and again.

TRY, ATTEMPT

The fists or "T" hands, palms facing each other, move forward and outward from the body in a parallel motion with the muscles tensed to indicate the expenditure of effort.

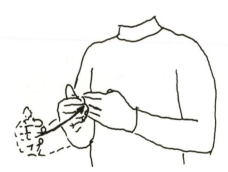

NEAR

The bent "B" hands are held, palms toward the body, the right hand farther away from the body than the left. The right hand is then brought toward the back of the left hand. Differing degrees of nearness may be indicated by the proximity with which the right hand approaches the left. VERY NEAR may be indicated by bringing the right hand in contact with the back of the left. NEAR + the PERSON MARKER = NEIGH-BOR. The sign may also serve as a verb. COME NEAR, APPROACH.

Table 10.2 Manual Concepts (Continued)

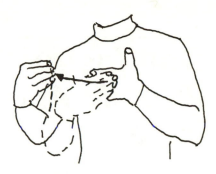

RIGHT

The right "R" hand, pointing upward, is moved off to the RIGHT from the body. For LEFT the left or right "L" hand is moved off to the LEFT from the body.

COPY, IMITATE

The left hand is held in a horizontal plane with the palm facing the body, and the finger tips of the right "5" hand touch the back of the left hand and then move away from the body as the thumb and fingertips come together, ending in the "And" configuration. A different sign is used for MAKE A COPY: the left hand is held with the palm facing the right, fingers pointing forward, and the right, "5" hand is drawn toward the left palm, ending in the "And" configuration as the fingertips and thumb of the right hand strike and the left palm. Instead of facing the right, the left palm may be directed outward or toward the object or material to be copied.

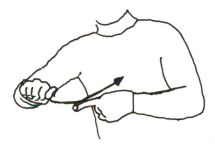

THROUGH

The right hand, palm up, is passed between the middle and fourth fingers of the left hand, which faces right. The sign translates the English preposition, THROUGH, but in some contexts it may stand as a verb, GO THROUGH. The left hand provides the point of reference, and the action of the right hand with respect to the left suggests meaning.

PRACTICE, TRAIN

The index finger of the left hand is pointed to the right, palm toward the body, and knuckles of the right "A" hand are brushed back and forth along the top of the extended index finger as the "A" hand is moved back and forth.

Table 10.2 Manual Concepts (Continued)

CHAPTER 11

Golf Instruction For The Visually And Hearing Impaired

by DeDe Owens

Visually Impaired

Larzo, a blind golfer and former National Amputee Champion, feels that golf instruction for the blind is no different than for sighted golfers. The swing techniques are the same (Chapter 3 and 4), however, the communication of the information requires a different emphasis.

Most sighted golfers are highly "visual learners." They learn by watching or modeling from a very early age. As such, modeling or demonstration (video, movies, T.V., graphs, pictures, etc.) is a very strong and effective instructional tool. It reduces the need for unnecessary verbiage. Unfortunately, as a result, instructors have grown overly dependent upon visual input as the source of learning, with less emphasis on the other four modes—auditory, tactile, kinesthetic and verbal. It is within these modes that the visually impaired must learn. For an instructor, this may necessitate a change in instructional orientation and raise an awareness level of the other modes of communication.

To prepare for teaching the visually impaired, it may help to simulate a golf experience in which your eyes are covered with a blindfold. Have a friend turn you in a circle several times, not to induce dizziness, but to induce a temporary loss of orientation and a dependency upon that friend for guidance. Make some practice swings with the club, then hit a few practice balls. Note your reactions to the experience both from a physical and psychological perspective. If you have had little experience in golf, the degree of uncertainty may be increased. Try to place yourself in the blind golfer's position. It is of course impossible to do, but perhaps it can help you gain some appreciation of the need to develop an awareness of other ways to communicate.

The suggestions for a golf unit for the visually impaired closely follow the progressions for the mentally retarded, with the same initial

purposes. They are to
- develop success patterns in club-ball contact immediately
- develop an awareness of an arm swing, body follow motion for later club control.

Whereas the emphasis for MR instruction is in modeling and demonstration, the emphasis for the visually impaired is tactile-kinesthetic and verbal, as discussed in the preceding section. Clarity in graphic exploration coupled with purposeful and directed manipulation is critical in the initial stages of learning the swing. Student-instructor feedback related to movement expectancy and outcome is likewise critical. Constant comparisons greatly enhance the learning process.

A BEGINNING GOLF UNIT
FOR THE VISUALLY HANDICAPPED*

by Diane Baxter
Physical Education Instructor, University of Oregon
LPGA Teaching Professional, Eugene, Oregon

Golf is a leisure activity for all people. The visually handicapped are no exception. This unit is designed on a one on one relationship with daily instruction over a period of three weeks.

Teaching and learning processes are fundamentally the same for sighted students; however, a few adaptations are necessary in methods and equipment. Learning will be at a slower pace since visual stimulation cannot be employed to aid in imitating movement patterns. Primarily the instructor will need to use meaningful words or expressions and avoid relying on gestures as an aid in giving directions and explanations. Demonstrations of the swing or stroke are replaced with the instructor or an individual assisting the student through the movement patterns. An individual not having sight is more sensitive to physical contact; therefore, actual manipulation of the student's body should be avoided.

An additional consideration is the equipment. It should be increased beyond the usual wood, iron, putter, mat and practice balls to include as many related items as possible (bag, cart, shoes, glove, etc.). A table displaying this equipment should be set up for each class period. To aid the student in comprehending a more complete understanding of the game, place on the table three models illustrating:
- a single golf hole
- three holes
- a nine hole course.

The models can be constructed using cardboard layouts with different textured paper and cloth materials to identify the tee, fairway, rough, sand traps and green. Toothpicks can be used as out-of-bounds stakes and flag poles. The models can be as elaborate as one wishes using frilled paper as trees and bushes or balsa wood for

---

*Reprinted with permission of the NGF.

benches or golf carts.

Special equipment needs are:
- VV Grips: A molded slip-on grip—allows student to attain correct grip easily and insure square club face.

- Tee-off Practice Aid: 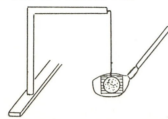 Apparatus consisting of a metal rod in a 90° angle standing upright from which a plastic ball is suspended on a small length of rope. When struck with the club, the ball and rope rotate around the rod, returning to hitting position.

- Toe Guide: Wooden stick anchored on a mat paralleled to the target line. (aids in alignment to ball and target.)

- Putting Guide: Two 1″ × 1″ × 4′ piece of wood, set a putter's head length apart, and held in place with cross pieces at each end.

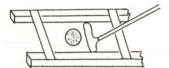

Suggested teaching aids are:[1]
- Artist mannequin
- Models of a golf hole and course

LESSON 1:
Introduction: The natural action of all people is to become oriented to a new area. An individual having sight does this unconsciously in a matter of seconds hundreds of times daily through visual observation. The visually handicapped individual's process naturally is different; it is often referred to as "trailing," the act of feeling objects in an area such as chairs, tables, walls, etc. As a means of acquainting the students to the instructional area and the equipment to be used, the first thing to occur is an orientation (trailing) of the space and equipment.

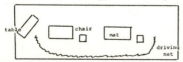

1. Each individual should develop his own teaching aids in relationship to his individual instructional unit.

The illustration shows the equipment table, driving areas with mats and one chair adjacent to each mat. The purpose of the chair is to have an object in the instructional area as a means of space orientation.

Once the class has moved to the golf course or activity field, the instructor will need to repeat the tailing process in the immediate instructional area and may also want to pace off a distance of approximately twenty yards in order for the students to be aware of how far the ball has traveled.

Equipment table—models of golf hole and course. Give brief description of the game.

LESSON 2:

Equipment table—putter, iron and wood. Discuss the difference of design and use in the game.

Individual movement exercises: Emphasize balance and rhythm.

- Body Swings—feel inside stride position (golf stance), arms stretched over head. Swing arms to right and down, touching floor in front of feet, lift up and back to over head position. Repeat reversing direction.
- Leg Swing—stand on one foot, swing non support leg forward and back. Use buddy for balance support. Repeat with opposite leg and swing leg across in front of body.
- Elephant's Trunk Swing (p. 7, Golf Instructor's Guide, National Golf Foundation).
- Partner Club Swing (p. 9, Golf Instructor's Guide, National Golf Foundation).
- Pendular Swing (p. 10, Golf Instructor's Guide, National Golf Foundation).
- Shoulder Turn—sitting on foot stool, place club on shoulders and behind neck, grip hands, palm forward at end of club—twist shoulders to right and back to left as far as they will turn.

LESSON 3:

Equipment table—clubs with VV Grip and artist mannequin

Repeat Exercises—emphasize balance, footwork and transfer of weight, begin to restrict unnecessary head movement.

Introduce: Grip, stance and alignment to target. Use mannequin to show body posture, ball placement. (NOTE: Most visually handicapped will "square off" [face a sound]. Have sighted partner align to target and talk allowing the visually handicapped to square off to partner. Toe board or guide will be helpful, too.)

LESSON 4:

Equipment table—tee-off practice aid

Repeat Exercises—(perform as many as possible in golf posture).

Review grip, stance and alignment

Introduce: ¼ swing—use practice aid and short iron.

LESSON 5:

Equipment table—golf bag

Repeat Exercises

Review ¼ swing—stress footwork and rhythm.

LESSON 6:

Equipment table—golf cart

Review exercises using golf club

Introduce: New exercises—towel; cane; firm, taut, control; control; isometric

Increase ¼ swing to ½ swing—use practice aid.

LESSON 7:

Equipment table—golf shoes and glove

Review Exercises

Increase ½ swing to full swing.

LESSON 8:

Equipment table—starter set of clubs

Review Exercises

Practice full swing—using different clubs and practice aid.

LESSON 9:

Equipment table—hitting mat, rubber tee, plastic practice balls

Warm up with selected exercises

Practice full swing—wood, mid-iron, short iron-use plastic practice balls

Review addressing ball, stepping away between every two or three hits.

LESSON 10:

Equipment table—model of golf hole—explain

Playing procedure—tee off, fairway shot, approach

Set up three stations—#1 wood full swing; #2 mid-iron full swing; and #3 short iron ¼ swing. Students rotate around stations hitting one or two shots at each station. Check alignment and address.

LESSON 11:

Equipment table—putter, cup liner, flag and pole, and model of putting green.

Introduce pendular putting stroke — stress balance, rhythm and smoothness.

Practice stroke with toe of putter trailing baseboard of wall — use books as stop guides for backswing and follow through.

Practice putting with hard ball using putting guide for stroke control.

LESSON 12

Equipment table—model of putting green, explain etiquette and rules.

Practice putting balls different distances—emphasize length of swing to distance of putt

Devise putting game.

LESSON 13:

Equipment table—models of golf hole, green and course layout.

Review game and playing procedures and etiquette.

Introduce: Selective basic rules

Review and practice full swing, ¼ swing and putting stroke.

LESSON 14:

Design 3 hole indoor course.

Orientation: Develop cardboard model of three hole course. Use model to show student distance, direction of hit and location of ball. (Same idea as used on TV with major tournaments.) Play using practice balls.

LESSON 15:

Set up 3 hole outdoor course.

Orientation: Same design as indoor course. Keep course short. Play using plastic balls or if area and skill permits, use hard balls. Use model of layout to indicate location of ball and hole.

Whenever possible, the visually impaired should be taught with a sighted partner. The partner becomes an active member of a team who provides the visual input in future course play by providing hole descriptions, target alignment and yardage. And the partner is critical from a safety standpoint. The unit should be modified to fit the needs of the individual student.

Hearing Impaired

Golf instruction for the hearing impaired follows the same instructional model (Chapter 4 and 5) as their non-impaired peers. However, special emphasis should be given to visual learning with less verbalization.

The instructor should be aware of the best means of communicating with the students—sign language, modeling, lip reading, or combinations. As indicated in the previous section, it may be necessary, and encouraged, that key signs be learned.

Safety for the student during instruction and on-course play is a major concern. Prior to beginning instruction signals should be established which indicate a warning as "stop" or "look out." The student should be in a position where the instructor, particularly the instructor's face, is always visible. The student may want to experience different positions as at the end of the instructional formation or the middle. The more severe the impairment, the more critical the visual contact. If the students are wearing hearing aids, many turn the volume down to reduce the "noise" or interference. This becomes a communication as well as safety concern. On-course play should be partner-oriented to insure safety for the students.

When working with the hearing impaired it is often felt that it is necessary to talk louder, to get extremely close, and/or exaggerate the lip motion when talking. It is just the opposite. The examples cited could produce confusion in communication or bring unnecessary attention to the student(s). The student-teacher relationship becomes very important. Establishing the groundwork for instruction to best meet the needs of the student is critical.

CHAPTER 12

Golf Instruction For The Physically Impaired

by DeDe Owens

Individuals with physical impairments will perhaps compose the larg-est single group of special populations interested in learning to play golf. The teaching progressions outlined in Chapter 4 and 5 and the communication model in Chapter 7 are important and appropriate in working with this group. As such, they will not be discussed further in this chapter. However, a review of these chapters is suggested.

The major focus of golf instruction for an individual with a physi-cal impairment is on the efficiency of motion. Efficiency is defined here as the ease of motion in the swing and the maximum use of one's individual swing potential. It is important for the instructor to have an understanding of the laws, principles and preferences of the golf swing in order to understand efficient motion. The priniciples with a variety of interacting preferences provides an instructor with numerous options for helping an individual adapt the golf swing to meet his particular needs.

Each individual has strengths and weaknesses of motion poten-tial which must be considered in order to determine the most efficient swing style (see Chapter 3 for a description of classical, classical-modern, and modern swing styles). Two motion factors should be considered: stability and mobility of the lower body, and upper body mobility. These two factors are particularly important in amputees, and will be discussed in this chapter.

Stability

Based upon the mechanical principles of movement, there should be few limitations in either stability or lower body motion for those indi-viduals whose physical impairment is restricted to the upper body. However, those individuals with lower body impairment may expe-rience motion restriction due to stability. The extent of the problem depends on the degree and location of impairment. For example, lower limb amputees may experience stability problems in the lower

Figure 12.1   **This young man shoots in the 80's and played on his high school golf team (courtesy of Clifford Owen, *Potomac News*).**

body whereas upper limb amputees would not. More specifically, below the knee (B/K) amputees have less stability problems than the above the knee (A/K) amputees.

Upper Body Movement

The second mobility consideration pertains to the upper body. Motion and swing control should be considered together in terms of range, consistency and force potential. An individual whose physical impairment is on their side closest to the target (i.e. left side for a right-handed golfer) or the reverse (right side for the left handed golfer) is capable of the greatest swing motion because of the greater swing radius. However, because of the greater swing radius, there is greater potential for inconsistency. In contrast, individuals whose physical impairment is on the rear side (side away from the target) have less swing motion, but tend to have more consistent control. Those individuals with full movement of both arms (such as leg amputees) are capable of increasing or decreasing the swing motion of the arms without loss of control.

An understanding of the motion capabilities and limitations of physically impaired individuals should enhance an instructor's ability to apply the swing preferences (Chapter 3) to these individuals. One swing style (classical, classical-modern, or modern: Chapter 6) is not necessarily efficient for all golfers. The classical swing style provides for more use of the upper body in a rear side dominant swing action with restrictions in the lower body. The classical-modern style emphasizes a swing motion incorporating more of the body as a functional unit (upper and lower body) with neither target or rear side dominance. The modern swing is power oriented. In the modern swing, the upper body creates a coiling action on the backswing to produce tension which is unleashed on the forwardswing by a strong leg driver (Chapter 3).

Flexibility in the application of the principles demonstrated by the three swing styles allows for the modification of swing patterns necessary to met the individual needs of physically impaired individuals. Since motion potential is the primary determinant of style preference, the following are suggested for instructing physically impaired individuals. The recommendations relate to the advantages and disadvantages of specific preferences in establishing motion and control.

The following recommendations are directed specifically to amputees for the purpose of continuity. They are applications of Wiren's model and its application for instruction discussed in Chapter 4. However it is important to note that these recommendations may be applied to other physically impaired individuals (i.e. neurological disorders, lower back problems, stroke, polio, etc.) that may exhibit similar strengths and weaknesses of motion potential. This is a

Figure 12.2   Former A/K champion, Dale Morgan. (Courtesy of *Golf World Magazine*).

beginning point or suggested baseline from which instruction may begin. Each individual requires unique considerations.

Instructional Recommendations For Lower Body Amputees

The lower body amputees as a group are more restricted in leg motion than the upper body amputees. Lower body amputees may be divided into two groups: below the knee (B/K) and above the knee (A/K) amputees. The B/K amputees should be capable of lower body motion with few restraints. As previously indicated, stability should not be a problem for the B/K amputees. Generally speaking, the preferences indicated for the classical-modern and modern swing styles should be more applicable for the B/K amputees in view of their motion potential than the classical style.

The A/K amputee may have a stability problem in weight bearing. Specifically, this would relate to the preswing principles of stance, ball position, target-rear foot weight distribution, heel-toe weight distribution, alignment (feet, hips, shoulders) and upper body posture at address. The preswing set-up directly influences the potential for inswing motion.

A recommended objective of the preswing for A/K amputees is to establish an address position that allows a free arm swing and takes into account a restricted lower body pivot or turning action. Some degree of lower body motion should be encouraged, but too much would result in lost motion. A brief explanation of the possible stabilizing preswing preferences and the related influences on the inswing principles can provide additional insight. A summary of the recommended preswing preferences is presented at the end of this section.

Stance

The stance provides the base of support for the swing motion. The stance should accomplish two things:
- provide for stability
- allow for motion

A stance which is too wide (more than shoulder width) tends to restrict lower body motion. The motion of the upper body would then also be restricted or become forced. A restricted or forced action is ineffective and may be the result of an inappropriate stance. The opposite extreme, too narrow a stance, can also produce a restricted or forced swing motion. For the A/K amputees, the individual must establish a compromise between the extremes which would allow for a pivot in the lower body with moderate weight transfer. The stance must support the swing motion of the upper body.

Figure 12.3 Sequence of Frank Cothran, former National Amputee Champion.

Weight Distribution On The feet

The initial weight distribution at address (with respect to either the target or rear foot) should be dictated by the amount and type of swing motion desired. The proponents of the rear side weight distribution at address suggest that it allows an easier and fuller turn with less tension on the backswing. The rear side weight position should encourage a free arms swing motion. Those favoring the weight initially set on the target foot endorse a swing which creates tension through the upper body (coiling action) by restricting the lower body on the backswing. However, this requires a strong let thrust on the forward swing in order to support the upper body release.

A rear to even weight position at address is recommended because it allows an easier turn on the backswing and forwardswing. This even weighting creates enough motion in the turn to support the upper body swing and still maintain balance. It is suggested that A/K amputees play with the amputation on the target side. The muscles in the stump can be used to help stabilize the weight transfer on the forwardswing. The rear side A/K may prefer to have more weight on the target foot because of the stability factor. However, this could reduce the total swing motion and create an excessive amount of tension in the swing. As a result, a less effective motion may be produced.

Heel-Toe Weight Distribution And Upper Body Posture At Address

Heel-toe weight distribution and upper body posture at address tend to influence each other. Weight distribution on heels is consistent with a more erect body position. Weight held towards the balls of the feet is consistent with a body position bending over the ball. Too much weight on the heels with an erect body posture produces a body oriented swing action with less arm freedom in the swing. A body oriented swing causes excessive hand action in the swing, and consequently the swing arc becomes flatter. The weight transfer tends to be less efficient and stability is often lost.

A position with the weight on the balls of the feet, and the body at an angle over the ball, encourages a free arm swing and weight transfer. There is less body restriction as well as a more efficient and easier swing motion.

The A/K amputee must establish a balance in weight distribution which is compatible with the posture position. The restriction in the lower body motion necessitates a free arms swing to maximize the upper body motion. Therefore, a position over the ball should be encouraged. However, if too much weight is toward the balls of the feet, stability is reduced. If too much weight is toward the heels, motion is reduced. Therefore, regardless of the side of the amputation (target/rear side), it may be suggested that an even weight distribution on the nonaffected side would permit stability and a free arm swing.

Alignment

The alignment of the body (feet, hips, shoulders) in relation to the target has a direct influence on the swing pattern and motion. The alignment of the feet and hips enhances or restricts the lower body motion. The shoulder alignment enhances or restricts the upper body motion and influences the swing arc and plane.

The A/K amputee is already restricted in lower body motion and should therefore avoid an open stance in the lower body. A closed

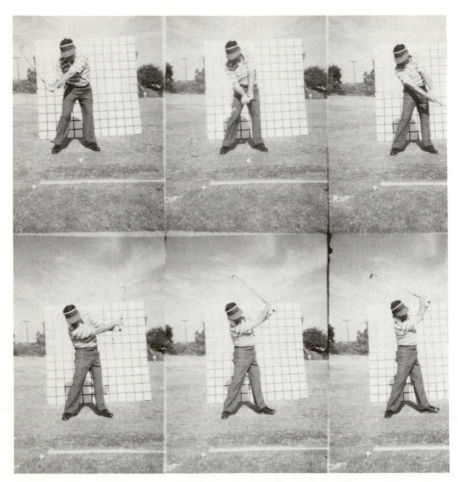

Figure 12.4   Sequence of Bill Hardy, former National Amputee Champion.

foot alignment and a square hip alignment are recommended for both target and rear side A/K's. This position allows better lower body motion (turn or pivot) in the backswing and in the forwardswing.

A square shoulder alignment helps to keep the clubhead swinging on the desired path for a longer period of time. This reduces the necessity of clubhead manipulation by the hands and encourages a free arm swing. The swing arc will also tend to be longer and more upright as opposed to flat (as a result of a closed shoulder alignment). An open shoulder alignment restricts the upper body motion and the length of the swing arc. Control may be gained, but distance will be sacrificed. Therefore a square shoulder alignment would be recommended for the A/K's to create as much freedom of motion as possible with control in the upper body. This tends to minimize the limited motion in the lower body.

Ball Position

The ball position in the stance influences the type of motion (hand or arm) and enhances or restricts the amount of swing motion. A ball position back of center in the stance encourages the classical style swing motion with rear side dominance and a flailing hand action. The lower body action is restricted, with the uper body lunging forward. The body finishes in a position in front of the target foot. This particular swing style is contraindicated for the A/K. The wider stance of this style when combined with the flailing hand action, reduces the needed swing control and stability of the lower body.

A ball position that is centered or forward of center would enable the A/K to utilize a more desirable arm swing for control and balance. Hand action is important in the golf swing. However, it should be the result of the arm motion and not because of a hand oriented flailing action.

Summary—Lower Body Amputees

Lower body amputees (A/K and B/K) care capable of an efficient swing. The swing preferences of the classical-modern swing style (with the specifically noted preferences) are more appropriate for the A/Ks. The B/Ks should experience few restraints and should be encouraged to create lower body motion. The classical-modern and modern swing preferences are appropriate for the B/Ks. The following instructional recommendation for lower body amputees are summarized from this section:

The B/K amputees should be capable of implementing the swing preferences of the classical-modern and modern swing styles.

The A/K amputees are capable of implementing the swing preferences of the classical-modern swing styles with consideration given to the following preswing principles and suggested preferences:

- Stance—The A/K amputees should avoid extreme stances of too wide or too narrow. Each individual must find a compromise in the width of the stance which allows for some degree of motion (pivot or turn) to support the upper body swing action.
- Target-Rear Foot Weight Distribution—A rear to even weight distribution would be recommended for the A/K amputees. This weight distribution encourages free motion on the backswing and support of upper body motion on the forwardswing.
- Heel-Toe Weight Distribution and Upper Body Posture at Address —A weight distribution which is even to forward, with an upper body posture over the ball, is recommended for the A/K amputee. The two positions are compatible and should encourage a free arms swing and lower body motion.
- Alignment—An alignment position in which the feet are closed and the hips and shoulders are square is suggested for the A/K amputees.

Figure 12.5   Backswing position of Cathy Boubel (B/E Amputee).

- Ball Position—A center to slightly forward ball position is recommended for the A/K amputees. This position encourages an arm swing motion and some degree of lower body action.

Instructional Recommendations For Upper Body Amputees

The upper body amputees must be considered from a different perspective than the lower body amputees. The lower body amputees have restricted lower body motion, but demonstrate freedom in the upper body because of the full use of both arms. The upper body amputees are the reverse. They demonstrate freedom in the lower body, but have restrictions in the upper body.

The subgroups within the upper body amputees: above the elbow (A/E) and below the elbow (B/E), may be considered together with respect to the swing principles. There are, however, differences between the target and rear side upper body amputees which have definite implications for instruction.

The development of a controlled and consistent swing is the prime objective of any golfer. For the upper body amputee, this may require more effort due to the lack of a support lever which potentially produces force and should provide control within the swing.

The rear side amputee has fewer control problems than the target side amputee. The rear side amputee is the closest example of a human two-lever model of the golf swing.

In general, the model swing concepts of target side control can be well illustrated by the rear side amputee's golf swing. To compensate for the absence of the rear side limb, complete adherence to the modern swing style principles cannot be recommended since a few adaptations must be made in order to permit more control. The classical-modern style would be more applicable for the majority of rear side amputees.

The target hand position with three knuckles on top would be recommended for the rear side amputees. This top position produces a slightly flatter swing arc and cupped position at the top of the swing and allows for more wrist action through the impact area. With the additional wrist action, distance should be gained. It should be noted that excessive wrist action could reduce the arm swing and thereby lose the desired gain in distance and control. The square hand position demonstrated by the modern swing style is feasibile. However, it would require a great deal of arm strength to continually repeat the swing without undue fatigue.

The target side amputees present potentially the opposite problems related in control. Whereas the rear side amputees could be

Figure 12.6   Set-up position of Jimmy Nichols. He played in 13 U.S. opens.

classified as pullers because the swing force is in front, the target side amputees would be classified as throwers. These two actions are very different. The pulling action uses the support of the lower body in the swinging action. In the throwing action, movement of the lower body is minimized and the swing is dominated by the rear side upper body and flailing hand action.

In terms of efficiency and consistency, the pulling action is the preferred. The swing action of the target side amputee tends to lose control the farther the rear arm moves away from the body on the backswing. The swing arc is greatly increased by the arm action, but timing and consistency of contact become more difficult.

To gain swing control, one of the first considerations should be to shorten the swing arc. This may be accomplished through the pressing set-up. Variations in the alignment of the feet, hips and shoulders can enhance and/or restrict the motion of the upper and lower body. The closed foot alignment tends to encourage a fuller hip turn on the backswing. This increases rather than decreases the potential swing arc. A square to slightly open hip and shoulder alignment would reduce the swing arc and add more swing control. This would also tend to permit a better arm motion (extension) through impact. A forward ball position would also encourage a more controlled arm swing with better lower body support. The more the ball position is back of center, the less effective the arm swing action. This positioning produces a restricted lower body motion and a choppy hand oriented swing motion.

Summary—Upper Body Amputees

A golf instructor must decide which swing style will be the most effective for the upper body amputee golfer. For an amputee who is just learning to play golf, it is recommended that they learn the golf swing with the remaining arm on the target side because of the previously discussed advantages related to control in a pulling type of motion. A new amputee with golf experience should be encouraged to experiment (with supervision) with both styles because of previously established movement patterns. An understanding of the advantages of both styles should be communicated to the student. Because of the aforementioned swing considerations, the rear arm swing will take longer to learn and present the greatest initial frustrations. The final decision should always take into consideration the student's present and potential ability and interest.

The application of specific preferences is dependent upon the individual amputee regardless of the site of amputation. Consideration should be given to the amputee's previous golf experience when beginning instruction. The following instructional recommendations for upper body amputees are summarized from this section:

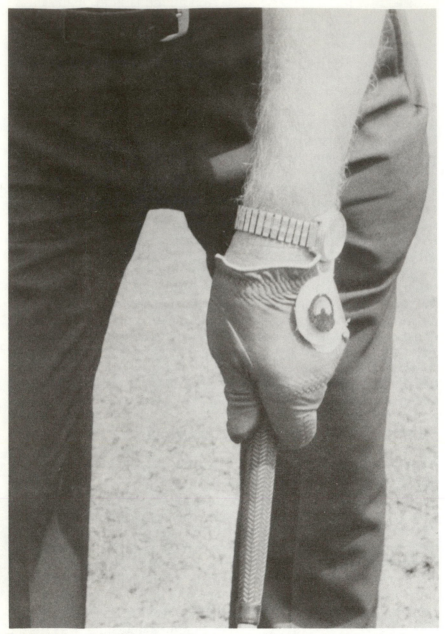

Figure 12.7   Target hand position recommended for rear side amputees.

The rear side amputee (A/E and B/E) has fewer control problems than the target side amputee (A/E and B/E); therefore the classical-modern swing preferences are applicable, with consideration given to the target hand position and resulting plane and position at the top.

- Target Hand Position—A top grip position is recommended for increased wrist action through impact.
- Plane—With the top grip position of the target hand, the plane will tend to be slightly flatter than that produced by a squarer grip position (upright plane).
- Position at the Top of the Swing—A cupped position at the top of the swing is recommended with the target hand grip position. A top grip position, a cupped position at the top of the swing, and a slightly flatter plane are compatible preferences.

The target side amputees need to be conscious of developing swing control by reducing the potential swing arc. The following swing preferences should be considered:

- Alignment—The alignment of the feet, hips and shoulders will help reduce the swing arc. A square to slightly open feet, hips and shoulders position will tend to decrease the swing.
- Ball Position—A center slightly forward ball position is recommended for a more controlled arm swing as opposed to the hand oriented action of a back ball position.

These recommendations are directed toward upper limb amputees playing golf without a prosthetic device. It would be suggested that B/E amputees play with a prosthetic device designed specifically for golf to enhance upper limb mobility and control. Above the elbow (A/E) amputees would probably find the prosthetic device to be of less benefit.

As instructors and non-impaired individuals we often take for granted our motion efficiency. What is it like to swing a club with one arm or standing on one leg? What adjustments and/or compensations must be made to accommodate for the loss of balance due to a missing arm or leg?

Understanding the mechanical principles and their implementation as a result of motion restricted in swinging a club is the beginning of golf instructions for the physically impaired. However, communicating the kinesthetic expectations in the swing motion and considering the student's capabilities and limitations will greatly enhance their learning process. Experiment swinging with one arm (right and left handed) and standing on one leg (right and left). Note the efficiency or lack of efficiency in the swing motion, strength factors, balance, special awareness, club control, ball contact and composure in execution. Your ability to demonstrate as needed with respect to limitations or loss of motion will facilitate your understanding of the student's needs and your ability to communicate.

PART 4

Conclusion

Psychological Considerations And Pleasure Of Teaching Golf To Special Populations

by Robert Rotella

Several years ago when I was dedicating most of my waking hours to becoming a successful collegiate athlete I would often become quite frustrated that I wasn't blessed with greater athletic talent. I believed I had done everything I could to increase my skills through practice, training and conditioning programs. I found myself constantly getting down on myself and questioning my ability to excel at sports in which I so badly wanted to be successful. I frequently wondered why so many others with much less interest and motivation were so blessed with greater talent.

Fortunately, my love for sport and exercise led to a summer job that involved teaching sport skills to mentally retarded, emotionally disturbed, socially deprived and physically handicapped children and adults. With each passing day it became more obvious that I was indeed very fortunate. I had been comparing myself to that small percentage of the population that was better off than myself. It also became apparent that these special people, despite their limitations, tried harder to improve themselves than any athlete I had ever known.

At the beginning of my teaching experience I had little knowledge about the special nature of the students I was about to teach. I showed up for work apprehensive, yet excited about teaching them everything I knew about sport. At first they questioned my sincerity. They wondered if I was committed to the time and energy it would take for them to learn.

They seemed to know that they could learn. They knew they were willing to be patient, but they didn't know about me. Their concern was that I would let them down as others had.

The program began with one brave student who was willing to try. Every few days a new student or two would ask to take part. Eventually they began to trust me and for the remainder of that first summer and the following six years I learned a great deal about the psychology of teaching so-called "handicapped" students. Hopefully, they learned a third as much from me.

Each day as I arrived at work I would find my students in a happy and enthusiastic mood, eager to learn. On the infrequent occasions when they did show up for class or practice in a slightly depressed state of mind, it was usually sadness related to someone else's sorrow or problem—seldom their own. I often wondered how these individuals could be so selfless and undeterred by their own handicaps.

With time I came to realize that these individuals were not unaware or blind to their difficulties. Rather, they had accepted their limitations. They had learned (either consciously or subconsciously) how to cope with their limitations. They had learned how to do the most that they could with what they were given. To my initial amazement, their performances in sport often far surpassed others with much greater talent.

Later, following my graduation from college, I coached high school basketball while continuing to teach special children during the school day. The players on my basketball team commented that it must take great patience to be able to teach special kids all day. I always responded in a similar fashion: "It doesn't take any patience at all to work with the retarded and handicapped. They all try too hard. What takes patience is working with young athletes like yourselves with all kinds of talent who fail to utilize it fully." I often reminded my athletes that whenever they felt discouraged they should look around until they found someone worse off than themselves. I encouraged them to try to learn to be happy with themselves and what they've got. I asked them to continually strive to develop themselves to their fullest potential.

Self-Perception: The Beginning Of Effectiveness

There is much more to attaining success in sport than having talent. Certainly it helps, but students' perceptions of their talent and the effectiveness of their approach to maximizing their potential may be more crucial. Athletes who have made themselves successful are not always the most gifted physically. Often there were obstacles in their way that could have easily prevented them from becoming successful. But their mental approach to learning and improvement allowed them to find success.

Bob Cousy and Phil Ford could easily have decided that they were too short to become great pro basketball stars. Chris Evert could have decided that she was too slow to become a great tennis star. Carlton Fisk could have become frustrated with his lengthy stay in the minor leagues and never allowed himself to become the top catcher in the American League. Fred Biletnikoff could have considered himself too slow to be a great receiver in the National Football League. Calvin Peete and Arthur Ashe could have decided that black athletes could not make it in professional golf or tennis. Nancy Lieberman could have decided that a woman couldn't develop great skill in basketball. Phil Mahre, the 1980 Olympic Medal Winner in Skiing, could have decided that there was no way he could return in a year's time from the terribly debilitating foot and ankle injuries he experienced within a year of the Olympic event. Carole Johnson was a finalist in the 1979 National Collegiate Gymnastic Championships, including a performance on the uneven bars, despite the congenital loss of her right arm at the elbow. She could have easily used her "handicap" as an excuse for failure or not trying. Instead she never perceived herself as even having a handicap. She simply had an obstacle that needed to be overcome. Charlie Boswell could have decided that a blind person couldn't become an outstanding golfer. In each case their teachers and coaches could have easily accepted the same self-limiting attitudes. Fortunately, they didn't. As a result we now have valuable role models.

There is a trait that appears to be common among individuals who manage to cope with the difficulties inherent in sport. *They perceive events in a way that increases their motivation* so they can find a solution to their problems and continue to work toward attaining their goals. The teachers must adopt the same attitude.

Learned Effectiveness
Since the time I first encountered these experiences, many years have passed. A theoretical approach to learning and teaching with practical application has evolved—a theory of learned effectiveness. Its implications suggest that there is a way to perceive and react to the world that will maximize effectiveness. Individuals who have learned effectiveness read their minds and bodies in a rational and realistic manner which allows them to attain their potential.

Rather than viewing a novel or unfamiliar learning or teaching situation with the view: "I can't do that," or "I doubt that I can do it" even before trying, individuals who have learned effectiveness approach the situation with the perception that "I can do it." Individuals who have learned effectiveness realize the importance of patience and persistence. They will have to be convinced otherwise before they believe that they can't. They persist even in the face of regular failure. They respond to failure by re-evaluating their practice strategies in a realistic manner, redesigning their approach and then increasing the intensity of their efforts.

When difficulties arise and improvement is slow, individuals with learned effectiveness actively seek out events in their environment which justify their continued efforts. They talk to others and read about others who have gone through similar experiences and have had their continued efforts rewarded. These people take great pride in the difficulty of the task that they are attempting. They appreciate and value their abilities no matter how meager. Where there are weaknesses they find a way through new knowledge or new strategies to overcome them. Less effective individuals emphasize that it's not fair when another person has more physical talent. More effective people focus on the fact that they are more dedicated and have more self-discipline than others.

Individuals who have learned effectiveness develop a great deal of pride in their mental and physical strengths. They give credit to their ability and their efforts when it will be helpful and lead to increased motivation. They are willing to give up responsibility for failure when doing otherwise would decrease their motivation.

People who have learned effectiveness take control of their lives. They realistically determine which activities will most effectively reward their efforts. They do everything possible to set themselves up for success rather than failure. To insure their success they accept responsibility for their success or failure. They do not let others destroy them or prevent them from attaining their goals.

Teaching the Handicapped

The opportunity to teach the game of golf to a person with a handicapping condition is an invitation to a challenging and rewarding experience. Perhaps some of your most successful strategies for teaching will no longer work. You may need twice the enthusiasm and persistence. You may even wonder whether or not you should waste your time teaching golf to a handicapped person.

Teachers without experience teaching the handicapped are in for a pleasant surprise. Many of your typical teaching techniques will be effective, with only slight adjustments. Contrary to your perceptions, you won't need half as much enthusiasm and persistence as usual. Many handicapped students will bring an excitement to learning and a willingness to practice seldom seen in other students. More than likely your efforts to be an exceptional teacher will be greeted with appreciation and thanks. You may love teaching such individuals so much that you will start wishing all of your students were "handicapped."

Eventually you will realize that your most important concern is to make certain that you don't waste one valuable moment of your students' time and energy. They try too hard to do anything less for them. With time, a sudden and new realization will occur—a handicap is only what a person makes of it. Individuals with handicaps may have their limitations but self motivation is not one of them. Indeed, it is their strength. They only need the direction and help of a skilled teacher.

An abundance of people typically considered "non-handicapped" are free of labeled limitations but are perceptually and motivationally handicapped. Who is happier? Who has more difficulties? Who will you get more enjoyment out of teaching?

Teacher Perceptions

There is much information that must be understood before a teacher can be as effective as desired when teaching. Nothing, however, is more crucial than viewing students with handicaps as being deserving and capable learners of the game of golf. You must look at the situation as a challenge that will help you test your teaching skills. It is an opportunity that will prevent you from stagnating.

Far too many teachers, young and old alike, will feel so uncomfortable about the possibility of teaching golf to the handicapped that they will run away from even trying. There are many excuses that teachers can come up with to rationally justify this escape. Such excuses may vary from a fear of the unknown to a fear of injuring students.

As we progress through this chapter, you will see that your students cannot afford the luxury of these highly ineffective ways of thinking. Teachers of golf can make their own life more meaningful by helping others receive the joy that they themselves have gotten out of golf. In turn their rewards for doing so will be twice as great.

A Self-fulfilling Prophecy

Teachers' expectations of their students are crucial to the speed and quality of learning that occurs. Expect great things of your students and chances are that students will come close to discovering their potential. Expect little from your students and you are just about guaranteed that they will fall short of their maximum ability level.

In their process of adjusting to their life condition, individuals must learn to focus on positive aspects of their limitations. Teachers must also learn to focus on their strengths and build upon them. In reality this is no different than the way effective teachers approach each of their students.

For the most part, this is how handicapped students desire to be treated—just like anyone else. They don't want special treatment. But they do and should expect their teachers to have the skills necessary to teach them effectively. They expect that what their teachers don't know they will find a way to learn.

Sympathy vs. Empathy

It is easy for many teachers to begin to feel sympathetic for students with handicapping conditions. These feelings and reactions must be resisted.

It is, however, advantageous to be empathetic. Strive to understand what it is like to be handicapped. Teachers who are not handicapped themselves will find it difficult to fully understand the experience, but they must try. (Teachers can learn a lot by trying themselves to simulate handicapping conditions while playing golf—you'll be surprised how much you can learn.)

Empathy, or the ability to put oneself in the person's place, will allow teachers to be more effective in meeting the goals of their students. Sympathy will most often cause teachers to lower their expectations for the student, as well as the students' goals. Students do not need pity. They need a teacher who will inspire them to greater heights. They need a teacher who appreciates their uniqueness, but wants to help them move onward and upward.

As any teacher of golf knows, there will be many frustrations and discouragements for any student. Sympathy will lead to the student and teacher feeling sorry for themselves. Empathy will lead to the teacher and student working together to overcome the obstacles that stand in their way. It is the only way that teachers can learn to fully understand their students.

Understanding A Crisis

Individuals with handicapping conditions may have come from two very different origins: they may have been born with a handicap or incurred some traumatic event later in life that resulted in their present condition. Either way, golf instructors can play a most significant role in the individual's adaptation to their condition. For individuals who were born with the handicapping condition, or incurred the condition early in life, chances are that they have made many of the adaptations about to be discussed. Their parents more than likely played a very influential role in teaching them how to deal with their situation. Hopefully, their teaching encouraged a positive and growth-oriented outlook. If not, you are in a situation where you can help a great deal if you know how. Your expertise and willingness to help individuals grow through the medium of golf may prove crucial to their continued mental, physical, and social adjustment.

Typical Responses To Injury

When an individual incurs a tramatic change (i.e., a handicapping condition) as a result of an injury they will typically advance through a series of adaptive responses. Five such stages, initially identified by Elisabeth Kübler-Ross (1969) can be anticipated:

- disbelief, denial, isolation, and as awareness of the extent of the injury grows—
- anger
- bargaining
- depression
- acceptance and resignation while continuing to remain hopeful.
  Instructors must anticipate and expect these responses from

students who are still adjusting to their handicap. They should remind themselves that these adaptive stages are both necessary and beneficial to the future well being of the individual.

Teaching Students To Think Rationally

The perception of many students with handicapping conditions is often inaccurate, especially if their responses to their condition are still emotionally based. These emotionally-based responses are usually influenced by conscious assumptions, evaluations and interpretations of situations. Handicapped students may feel sorry for themselves, anxious, guilty, or depressed because they feel that it is "awful" or "catastrophic" that they are handicapped. Their emotional responses may intensify if they begin to fear that they will be rejected or ridiculed by peers or teachers. Soon they may begin to think that they are unimportant or useless human beings. The emotional reactions to these thoughts may interfere with the teacher's success at teaching golf.

Psychological Implications

Each individual with a handicapping condition must learn to adjust to social demands as well as to his own personal limitations. The necessary adjustments present a serious challenge which may cause handicapped students to experience more frequent and serious psychological problems than students who are not handicapped. Of course, it is this very same situation that may cause many handicapped students to develop far greater levels of self-motivation, persistence, and coping ability than others. The handicapped students' success at adjusting to their handicaps is determined by a combination of individual personality, family influences, and peer and teacher influences.

Family Influences

Parents who set unrealistically high expectations for their children tend to have children who are constantly frustrated and left unsatisfied with their accomplishments. Parents who set unrealistically low expectations for their children are inclined to develop handicapped children lacking in the motivation to attempt an activity as challenging as golf. Teachers who recognize such students, must be willing to actively and enthusiastically encourage these students to get involved in golf. There must be a willingness to turn them on until they develop the necessary self-confidence to encourge themselves.

The impact of a handicapped child on a family is monumental. The child may influence the parents' perceptions of themselves which may greatly affect the way the parents react to the child.

Hopefully, parents will convey genuine love, warmth, and acceptance to their handicapped child. If not, psychological adjustment may suffer.

Most parents of the handicapped (much like their teachers) will struggle with the problems of dependence, independence and over-protection. For healthy development to take place, independence will be necesssary. Overprotection will only serve to prevent and/or minimize growth. Certainly it may appear to be less risky to allow a handicapped child to remain dependent upon the parents. However, the long term effects of this approach can be quite hazardous. The longer independence is delayed the more difficult it will be for the handicapped individual to manage. Parents must strive for the gentle balance between independence and dependence. It is a difficult but necessary task.

Whenever possible, children with a handicapping condition must be treated in a fashion consistent with other children. They must be given responsibilities and be expected to carry them out successfully. As with others, praise must be given to the handicapped when deserved; however, care must be taken to make sure that they are not given unwarranted attention. The parents' success at handling these difficult tasks will impact upon the child's success at living in the real world.

Raising a handicapped child may place strain upon family interactions. Parents having difficulty accepting the fact that they have a handicapped child may inadvertently vent their frustrations on other children in the family. Such behaviors may serve to isolate the handicapped child from siblings. Parents and siblings must appreciate their role in helping each child feel good about himself. They must learn to be proud of the accomplishments of the child rather than feel ashamed or embarrassed about the handicapped boy or girl.

School Influences

When a child with a limiting condition enters school, that child is likely to be uncertain as to whether he will be accepted or rejected, treated as an equal or pitied and patronized. Certainly other students experience these same doubts, but a child with a handicap may feel particularly inferior when compared to non-handicapped students. This may be particularly true if previous social interactions have been lacking.

Teachers must help classmates accept and understand the feelings experienced by students with handicaps. Peer acceptance will be crucial to the learning accrued by the handicapped. Heartless and insensitive students may interfere with the development of the desired social skills. When peers do behave in an inhumane manner, teachers must find a way to help them better understand the handicapped student's situation and also help the handicapped student to learn how to respond to such insensitive individuals. They will face many others in their life ahead.

Self-Concept

Golfers with handicaps interact with many different individuals — family, peers, and teachers—each of whom contributes to the view taken of himself or herself. If the interpersonal reactions are generally positive then the likelihood of a positive self-image will be enhanced. If the experiences are mainly anxiety filled, chances are that the self-image will be negative, with the associated anxious feelings.

Teachers will have few problems with students who have a sense of self-worth. Without feeling good about themselves, all individuals have difficulty getting along with others. Success at teaching golf to these students will be particularly crucial to their healthy growth and development.

Teachers must help their students learn to enjoy the process of self-improvement rather than constant and direct competition against others. Competition against others should not be precluded, but should not be the most important goal. Each personal success at self-improvement has the potential for an increased self-image. Teachers must help provide such experiences for their students and then show them how to do the same in other aspects of their life.

Social Acceptance

Individuals who deviate in appearance from others may find themselves somewhat isolated. Teachers can help them by showing them strategies that can enhance the view that others hold of them. Individuals help their situation by realizing that many others value conforming behaviors. Dressing in a style consistent with others, sharing their interests in conversation, music, and recreation can facilitate their acceptance. Many students with handicaps are isolated due to social considerations in these areas, yet may inaccurately perceive that it is a result of their handicap rather than the other factors mentioned.

On the other hand, individuals with handicapping conditions cannot just become total conformists. They must be helped to understand when to be themselves and stand on their own and make their own personal decisions. Extreme and inconsistent behavior can lead to social and personal problems.

Golf As A Tool

Golf can become a most valuable tool for individuals with special considerations. Golf is a game that allows them to be competitive with even the non-handicapped. It is a game that can help the handicapped accept themselves and be accepted by others.

Through success at golf, many skills can be mastered: emotional control, goal setting, positive thinking, and acceptance of human limitations. Such learning will only occur if teachers teach these skills to their students. Later, students can be shown how these skills can be applied in other aspects of life.

To accomplish these objectives, teachers of the handicapped must be willing to serve as mediators betwen others and self direction. Initially, students may depend upon their teachers for encouragement and direction. Eventually students must be able to direct themselves and provide their own enthusiasm.

The Keys To Motivation

Finding a way to motivate each and every student is without doubt one of the most difficult and important responsibilities given to teachers. Teachers' effectiveness at enhancing motivation will greatly influence the success of their students.

Certainly success will not be determined entirely by motivation. But motivation is one very significant element of success that a teacher can influence. The solutions to student motivation will not always be found in science. But usually, effective motivation will depend upon a teacher's ability to artistically apply what is scientifically sound. There are several basic points crucial to an understanding of motivation. Teachers should be well aware of their importance.

Observe Actions and Moods—Perhaps the first key to becoming a skilled motivator is to become a master at observing the actions and moods of individual students. Teachers who carefully observe their students will quickly recognize that students act and feel in very idiosyncratic ways. They are not all the same and therefore all students will not be motivated equally by the same strategies.

Not all students will perceive a particular motivational strategy in the same manner. Once teachers realize there are perceptual differences among students, they can begin to analyze individual students and situations in a style that will allow them to become successful. They can begin to ask themselves: "Why is a certain student discouraged and walking with a hanging head?" "Is the student looking for attention?" "Does the student need attention or help from me?" "Should I be tender or should I tell the student to stop feeling sorry for himself (pick up your head and act like a winner)?" "Why is the student feeling depressed?" "Has the student been performing poorly?" "Did I just yell at the student?" "Did she just make an embarrassing error in front of the class?" "Did the student's parents just get divorced?" "Did the student just fail a test or get rejected by a preferred college?"

These questions are only a brief beginning. Obviously, to answer them a teacher needs to be knowledgeable and understanding. Certainly, teachers must really care about getting the most out of their students if they are going to do what is best for each student and to think of all the factors potentially influencing motivation.

The perceptual approach to motivation is undoubtedly effective but it does demand a commitment by teachers to spend time thinking

about the actions, feelings and thoughts of their athletes. A base of knowledge will be presented here to help:
- understand potential influences on motivations
- become familiar with effective motivational strategies.

Hopefully, when armed with this information, (i.e., intuition and common sense) teachers will be of more benefit to their students.

Opting for Optimism—Effective motivation will demand that a teacher opt for optimism. But optimism cannot be expressed only through words. Every action and behavior must suggest that a teacher is optimistic. Clearly, the students will model the teacher if they believe the teacher. They must believe. If the teacher's actions belie his words there is little chance that optimistic words will be accepted. Often this means that a teacher must be optimistic but realistic. Unattainable optimism may lead to frustration and/or a loss of faith in the teacher's leadership.

There is no doubt that it is sometimes difficult for teachers to be optimistic. It is next to impossible to motivate students to believe in themselves when things are going poorly if teachers refuse to believe in them. Teachers, like students, can lose confidence and become pessimistic when things are going poorly. Indeed, it is far easier to think pessimistically than it is to think optimistically at such times. Teachers cannot, however, expect their students to remain optimistic if they are not themselves.

Communication and Trust—Another key to motivation is to establish communication and trust with students. The initial meetings with students are often the most important for opening lines of communication (primary effect). Teachers facilitate communication when they are excited during their first contacts with their students. It is important that all students know that their teachers really enjoy teaching them.

As a result of this first interaction, students realize that the teacher cares about each student. This belief will persist as long as the teacher is receptive and interested when students request help. Many successful teachers believe that if they make an error in motivating students it should be as a result of trying too hard or caring too much.

Communication and caring cannot be easily faked. Teachers who do not truly care about their students will have a difficult time convincing them otherwise. There is little doubt that this point, at least in part, explains the fact mentioned in the previous chapter that great teachers are active listeners. They listen because they care. Because they care, they listen and use what they hear to help them motivate each and every student that they teach.

Non-Verbal Communication: Your Body Counts — Often a teacher's body language sends important messages to each and every student. Teachers must understand these messages. Experts in kinesics or non-verbal communication consider the impact of a message to be 55% body language. It is further believed by such experts that unless trained, the body does not know how to lie; thus, it is often emphasized that it's not what a teacher says, but how the teacher communicates that is important.

When the teacher walks into the practice area the initial greeting may be, "Okay, let's bring it in. I want a really good class today." But the way the teacher walks into the area (a confident, energetic stride, or a tired, bent over walk), the tone of voice (an enthusiastic and excited commanding voice or a pleading, whining voice), the look in the eyes (excited and wide open or uninterested and half asleep), and even the calm, comfortable, or enthusiastic movements of a teacher's arms and hands deliver messages.

Although body postures do not always deliver the same message, the meanings are often quite similar as long as the situation and the spoken words are understood. Even then, different students may interpret body language quite differently depending upon how they are feeling (e.g. nervous or confident) or thinking (teacher likes me or dislikes me).

Teacher Speaks In Monotone
depressed

uninterested

little interest in class

doesn't care enough to get psyched

teacher is mad

teacher is distracted by something
  that has happened outside of class

bored

teacher doesn't enjoy job

a superior attitude—
  "I am better and smarter than you"

Teacher Raises An Eyebrow In Response To A Student's Question
teacher disagrees

doesn't understand

confusion

it's up to you—there is nothing more
  I can do

thinking and/or analyzing your
  comments

just made a point that was of interest

surprise

"so you think you know more than I do"

Teacher Walks With Head Down
concentrating on new strategy

disappointment

lack of confidence

very serious—no nonsense

psyching self up for class

gathering thoughts

wondering what went wrong

a real bad day

teacher has given up on individuals or
  the entire class

Table 13.1 Interpretations Of Body Signals Sent By Teachers

Teachers aren't the only ones who send body signals. Students also deliver unspoken messages with their bodies. Often teachers misinterpret the body language of students.

Teachers must learn to accurately read the body messages sent from students and respond to them. If a teacher sees that a particular student's head is frequently hanging it may be a sign that the student needs some attention from the teacher. The teacher must know the student and the situation well enough to know the meaning of the body signal, or be smart enough to approach the student and inquire. Attending and responding to body signals will help teachers to understand and be capable of motivating all their students in a more effective manner.

Self-Directed Motivation—A final key to motivation emphasizes that one goal should always be to develop motivation that will become long-term and self-directing. It is true that not all students will, despite the best efforts, become self-directed. However, teachers should at least strive for it. When faced with this situation, a teacher's job is much like a parent's — to meet the needs of dependence and yet strive to prepare students for eventual independence. Fostering independence or self-directed motivation is often difficult for teachers to accept. Many teachers have a strong need to be needed. Teaching students to be capable of functioning without the teacher's help is an uncomfortable thought, but it must be the goal.

It is the student, not the teacher, who must compete, cope, adjust, and perform. Certainly the teacher can intervene during class and during practice, but during play students must be capable of self-motivation and direction.

Each student's success or failure at self-direction will be significantly based upon the teacher's wisdom and ability to teach self-motivaton. John Wooden, the famous basketball coach from UCLA, emphasized this point several years ago with his students. "It is important to remember that the preparation of an athlete is complete when the coach or teacher is no longer needed."

Teaching The Process Of Goal Setting

Students, whether handicapped or not, go through a consistent process as they make decisions about approaching or avoiding goals. This process must be understood prior to outlining a goal setting program.

When students are placed in a situation involving an achievement task (golf) they attempt to determine their chances of success (or failure) and whether or not the task is worth striving to attain. This self-analysis involves asking

- whether or not the necessary talent is available
- how much luck will be involved in success or failure
- how difficult is the task (cost and availability of instruction, equipment, practice facilities and practice partners)
- whether the effort required is worth it (personal and social rewards).

This very conscious evaluation of the task leads to an estimation or prediction of personal chances for success or failure. It is here that both expectancies for success and failure as well as the hope of success and the fear of failure are initiated for a specific task.

If the student decides to approach the task, then goal-directed behavior beings. The student formulates a plan or strategy for attaining success and avoiding failure. The student then goes about the process of carrying out the plan.

Next, the student must compete in the achievement situation (plays a round of golf). With each performance opportunity the student re-evaluates his plan and his progress. A self-appraisal and task appraisal is gradually formulated. The student must learn to totally believe in himself and in the effectiveness of the plan while remaining flexible enough to make adjustments in goals and plans.

These decisions are based upon a self-evaluation of why success or failure occurred. Was success or failure due to:

- ability or lack of the necessary ability?
- a willingness to put forth the necessary effort, intensity, and persistence, or the lack of a belief that effort plays any role in success or failure?
- being lucky or unlucky (or at least perceiving that success or failure was due to good or bad fortune)?
- the difficulty of the task (which may constantly change)?

The re-evaluation process that follows goal-directed behavior and performance leads to experiences of pride or shame, as well as expectancies of future success or failure. The importance of self-perception in this process has previously been discussed under learned effectiveness. Students must next be taught how to positively attack their weaknesses in practice so that they can think positively about them during play. This process can be facilitated by self-image psychology.

Teaching The Importance Of Goal Setting
Success in golf is often determined by setting goals and working

toward them. Effective goal setting is the first step in maximizing golf potential.

Setting a goal fulfills at least four important functions. It
- prepares students mentally and emotionally to act out their commitment
- expresses confidence
- creates a positive self-image that the student is in control of improvement and performance
- provides a focus of energy.

Goal setting should emphasize a process of striving for a goal that is challenging, yet attainable. Teachers must teach their students that it is the process of attaining the goals rather than winning or losing relative to others that is most important in golf. Successful teachers at the highest levels have emphasized this point. Even the famous Vince Lombardi quote was misinterpreted. His comments on his deathbed show his concern for the resulting abuse.

> Winning isn't everything, it's the only thing. I wish the hell
> I'd never said the damn thing. I mean the effort . . . I sure
> as hell didn't mean for people to crush human values
> and morality.
> (Michener, 1976, p. 432)

Goals must be realistic. But it's not always easy to determine whether a goal is realistic or impossible. For this purpose goals should include both long-term and short-term or intermediate goals. As each short-term goal is accomplished students will move closer to the attainment of the eventual long-term goal. If only long-term goals are set, goal setting may induce tension and frustration. Students need intermediate successes to build confidence and persistence.

Golf teachers must help their students in the goal setting process. (Table 13.2). Together, teachers and students may draw up a master list of all the skills required for reaching the desired goal (physical skills, conditioning, mental skills, etc.). The list should be very specific and should include practice suggestions for improvement in each area.

Next, teachers and students must detail in sequential order their skills from the weakest to the strongest. When this list has been completed, a specific amount of time must be allocated daily for practicing individual areas of weakness. As each student's weakest skill is improved, time is spent on the next weakest skill. Teachers should also make certain that students know what their strongest skills are and spend sufficient time maximizing these strengths.

Table 13.2
Setting Your Goals And Attaining Them

There are at least six steps which are crucial to the goal setting process:

Step 1 — Know Yourself

How good a golfer are you?

How good would you like to be?

Why in the past have you not progressed as you would like?

Are you self-disciplined?

Do you concentrate when you practice?

Are you willing to take responsibility for your achievement or would you rather blame others or bad luck for your success or failure?

Step 2 — Skills Required for My Sport

What are the skills required for success in golf?

Do you understand the strategies and rules in golf?

Do you understand the mental aspects of golf?

Do you know what muscle groups are utilized in golf and how to develop them?

Do you know which muscle groups must be relaxed to consistently perform effectively?

Do you have enough flexibility to perform up to your potential?

Step 3 — Self Evaluation

What are your greatest strengths as a golfer?

What are your greatest weaknesses in golf?

Do you know how to go about improving each of them?

How much time are you willing to put into practice?

Do you tend to practice only the shots you enjoy?

Are you practicing perfectly to ensure success or are you just putting in time?

Do you tend to practice your strengths or the skills you are already good at with very little time on your weaknesses?

Is the amount of time you spend on each skill related not only to what needs the most improvement, but also the skills which mean the most to success in your sport?

Step 4 — Define Your Goals

Define your goals. Be sure that your goals are challenging but realistic.

Be certain that if you put the time and effort planned into them that you will automatically raise your level of aspiration and raise your goals.

Step 5 — Plan

Plan how you will meet your goals.

How much time do you have to attain your long term goals?

How can you best use the resources at your disposal in the time you have to learn?

What will your plan of attack be for attaining each of your sub-goals?

How much will you attain each day, week, month, year?

Step 6 — Evaluate Your Progress

Evaluate your progress.

Are you programming effectively? Is your improvement on schedule?

Imagine The Accomplishment Of Goals

One way to enhance success is to program the system for success by constantly reminding the individuals of the goals and to imagine accomplishing them. Students should spend five to ten minutes per day imagining themselves accomplishing their goals.

The strategy of closing one's eyes and imagining successful completion of goals is called "mastery rehearsal." Psychologists are uncertain as to whether or not actual visual pictures in the mind are necessary. It may be just as useful to simply think about the attainment of goals even if a visual image does not appear. Either way, the system needs to be stimulated by success experiences on a regular basis. Structured mental practice on the part of each student is the best way to accomplish this task. It should, however, be constantly combined with confidence-enhancing statements by the teacher reminding each student that success will occur.

Conclusion

Teaching golf to students with handicapping conditions is one of the most challenging and rewarding tasks that any teacher will experience. There are no magic answers that will guarantee success for teachers or students.

Teachers must be willing to make a commitment to understanding the students and be patient in helping them through the many challenges to be faced.

Hopefully, golf can provide students with an activity that can allow them to interact with other people in a self-satisfying and confidence-enhancing manner. In this manner it is hoped that teachers of golf can help students with handicapping conditions become happier and more fully adjusted.

Teachers willing to accept the challenge of instructing the handicapped will eventually realize that they received more from the experience than their students. They will discover that the knowledge gained in learning to teach these students will make them more successful at teaching their other students.

References

Beck, A. "Cognitive Therapy: Nature and Relations to Behavior Therapy." *Behavior Therapy*, 1970, pp. 184-200.

Cruickshank, W., Ed. *Psychology of Exceptional Children and Youth.* Englewood Cliffs, New Jersey: Prentice-Hall, Inc., 1966.

Ellis, A. *Reason and Emotion in Psychotherapy.* New York: Lyle Stuart Press, 1962.

Fait, H. F. and Billing, J. E. "Reassessment of the Value of Competition." In *Issues and Physical Education and Sport*. G. H. McGlynn, Ltd., 1974.

Kessler, J. W. "The Impact of Disability on the Child." *Journal of the American Physical Therapy Association* 46 (1966): 153-59.

Kohut, S. A. "The Abnormal Child: His Impact on the Family." *Journal of the American Physical Therapy Association* 46 (1967): 160-67.

Kübler-Ross, Elisabeth. *On Death and Dying*. New York: The Macmillan Company, 1969.

Mahoney, M. J. *Cognition and Behavior Modification*. Cambridge, Massachusetts: Ballinger, 1974.

Meichenbaum, D. *Cognitive-Behavior Modification: An Integrative Approach*. New York and London: Plenum Press, 1978.

Michener, J. *Sports in America*. Random House, 1976.

Rotella, R. J. "Psychological Care of the Injured Athlete." In *Psychological Considerations in Maximizing Sport Performance*. Edited by L. K. Bunker and R. J. Rotella. The University of Virginia, 1981.

Rotella, R. J. and Bunker, L. K. *Mind Mastery for Winning Golf*. Englewood Cliffs, New Jersey: Prentice-Hall, Inc., 1981.

Bibliography

Bleck, E. E. and Nagel, D. H. *Physically Handicapped Children: A Medical Atlas for Teachers.* New York: Grume and Stratton, 1975.

Cratty, B. J. *Adapted Physical Education for Handicapped Children and Youth.* Denver: Love Publishing Company, 1980.

Johnson, C. and Johnstone, A. *Golf: A Positive Approach*, Reading, Maine: Addison and Wesley, 1975.

Martenuik, R. G. *Information Processing in Motor Skills.* New York: Holt, Rinehart and Winston, 1976.

Owens, N. D. *Analysis of Amputee Golf Swings.* Doctoral Dissertation, University of Virginia, 1980.

Rotella, R. and Bunker, L. *Mind Mastery for Winning Golf,* Englewood Cliffs: Prentice Hall, 1981.

Sherrill, Claudine. *Adapted Physical Education and Recreation.* Duburque: Wm. C. Brown, 1979.

Wheelen, R. H. and Hooley, A.M. *Physical Education for the Handicapped.* Philadelphia: Lea & Febiger, 1976.

Appendices

Appendix A.
Typical Golf Lesson Program

The basic program may consist of 5 one-hour sessions. A typical breakdown of the hour would be as follows:

Part 1 —20 minutes —Lecture
Part 2—10 minutes—Active participation
Part 3—30 minutes—Active participation

When working with various skill levels it is suggested that the teacher use expertise to slow down or speed up the progress. Even within the group, individual exercises and drills may be added to adjust to the progress level of the individual student. Don't be afraid to have a variety of skill levels working within the same class.

Lesson 1

Part A — 20 minutes
History, general club parts, ball flight laws.

Part B — 10 minutes
Grip choices, tension in grip.
Exercise—Two handed full turn; one handed wide-whoosher exercise; land 2 rhythm drill.

Part C — 30 minutes
Hitting balls (plastic or hard), teed up and with 5 or 7 iron. May check Ball Flight Laws.

Lesson 2

Part A
Terms.

Part B
Hand and arm drills—counter-clockwise club drill; palm down-palm up club drill. Review wide-whoosher drill.

Part C
Hitting balls—teed—with middle irons.

Lesson 3

Part A
Rules — suggest making a simulated golf hole layout on the floor and walking through the rules. Good visualization.

Part B
Approach Shot — introduce a clock analogy to emphasize the equal parts of the swing backward and forward. Show varied club effects from 5-pw.

Part C
Approach shot practice with 5-7-9 irons.

Lesson 4
Part A

Courtesies — before round, during and after. Suggest from pro shop to tee to the green.

Part B

Putting introduction and drills.

Part C

Putting practice—stroke and tap using various lengths of putts.

Lesson 5
Part A

Equipment—club selection—balls—clothing—shoes.

Part B

Review full swing—wood variation.

Part C

Hit full swings with irons and woods

When expanding basic lesson plans from 5 one-hour units to more sessions, such as 10 or 15, the following suggestions can be used to vary the plans. To add fun and variety use national Golf Foundation films and loops. A continued use of different drills and exercises to strengthen various areas of the swing may be added by using the *Instructors' Guide* and the *Coaches' Guide*, also put out by the National Golf Foundation. These manuals also contain many suggested ways for adapting facilities and class space.

Make it fun for all skill and age groups. Be sure to give your students much positive reinforcement.

10 Sessions		15 Sessions or More Skilled	
Lesson	Emphasis	Lesson	Emphasis
1	Full	1	Full
2	Full	2	Full
3	Full	3	Full
4	Short Approach	4	Short Approach
5	Approach-Ch. Speed	5	Approach-Ch. Speed
6	Putt	6	Putt
7	Play 3 Holes	7	Woods
8	Full-Woods	8	Play 3 Holes
9	Simulated Game	9	Basic Sand
10	Putting Game or on Course Scramble	10	Trouble Shots
		11	Full-Skill Tests
		12	Plastic Ball Course or Actual Play
		13	Long Irons or Woods
		14	Putting Games
		15	Play 9 Hole Scramble

Appendix B. Golf Instructional Aids

Aid	Purpose	Design
Putting*		
1.	1. To develop feel in a pendulum stroke (length adjustable) Distance Back = Distance Through	Two 2" x 2" boards, 2' long
Target Ball Blade	2. To develop blade awareness	Bore holes from the middle (to right and left) at the following intervals: 3", 2½", 2½", 2½"
	3. Self-corrector with different audio sounds if ball contracts off target (blade error) (Path of blade restricted) (visual/kinesthetic)	2" x 7" rods with nails at the ends
2.	1. Same as above without restricted path placed on floor or rug	Strips of tape 24" long
Target	2. To develop a feel for the varying lengths in the stroke with guides for blade alignment and length	Strips of tape 6" long
Full Swing	1. To develop a feel for body and club alignment to a target	Two strips of tape/cord ribbon 3' long
	2. To develop a feel for ball position	One strip of above 2' long or use three clubs or shafts without heads
	3. To develop a feel for distance from the ball and posture	
	4. To develop a method for alignment (visual/kinesthetic/tactile)	Add footprints with L/R or different textures for visually impaired or MR

Golf Instructional Aids

Aid	Purpose	Design
Chipping	1. Same as full swing 2. To develop an understanding and feel for the differences in posture and positioning in the short shot and full swing	Same as design for full swing aid
Posture Platform Designs		
1.	1. To develop a feeling of being back and behind the ball	3½′ square heavy plywood with ends of 2″ and 6½″
	2. To develop an understanding of posture and weight changes for specialty shots (up-down hill/sidehill) (visual/kinesthetic)	Rubber matting cover with a brush mat attachment for left and right handed golfers. It should be stable enough to hit balls on
2.	To develop a feeling of free arm hang, posture and swing center at address (visual/kinesthetic)	3′ x 6″ square heavy plywood
Indoor Wall Targets		
1.	To develop an understanding of club loft and trajectory (visual/kinesthetic/audio w/adaption)	Line 2′ above the floor
2.	1. To develop target awareness with club loft and trajectory (circle in square may reinforce academic work of MR's and young children)	Place with tape at point on a wall — circle 3′ diameter, square 9′ width
or		or
	2. To provide self-testing and motivation in practice	Same design as above with an additional circle with a 12′ diameter Audio Adaptions: Use contrasting sounds coverings for each area

Golf Instructional Aids

Aid	Purpose	Design
Model Golf Hole	To develop an understanding of hold design and terminology (visual/tactile)	1' x 2" plywood Three contrasting surfaces for rough/fairway/green and tee 30 toothpicks 10 yellow 10 red 10 white ½ square cloth for play Bore out traps and hazards for real sand and water Braille lettering of terms
Ball-Club Contact	To develop swing motion with ball-club contact (visual/kinesthetic/audio)	L-shaped rod mounted on a platform that can be stabilized (in or out of doors). Suspend a plastic ball by a cord
Arm And Hand Speed Streamer Club	To develop an understanding of arm and hand speed relative to acceleration and effects of centrifugal force (visual/kinesthetic/audio)	Tie streamer or ribbon to end of club — continuous motion streamers stay out in arc

Golf Instructional Aids

Aid	Purpose	Design
2. Wide "Whoosher" Drill	Same as streamer club (Swing club target arm only, holding at end of shaft by the head—generate speed)	Upside down club—acceleration makes "whoosher" sound
Molded Grip	To develop a feel for the grip position (visual/kinesthetic)	preformed by manufacturer
Trajectory	To develop a feel for the difference in club loft and resulting ball trajectory (visual/kinesthetic)	Mount clubs (1,3,5 woods, 3,5,7,9 P.W., SW irons) on a board 5" apart, beginning with the less lofted club on the left (righthanded/reverse for lefthanded set). Bore a hole, one to the loft of each club. A 12" rod should fit the hole. An adaptation with a plastic, flexible tubing 24" long and attachable to the rod will establish the desired parabolic trajectory

*1 and 2 are developing stroke technique, not distance awareness.